COLLECTING AMERICAN VICTORIAN ANTIQUES

COLLECTING AMERICAN

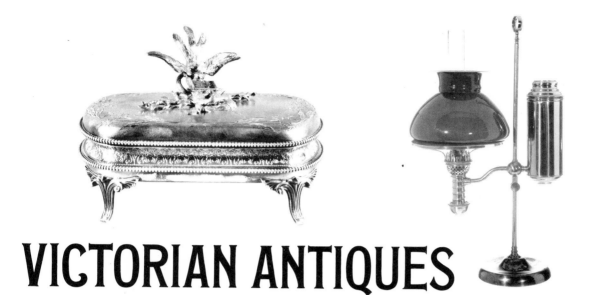

VICTORIAN ANTIQUES

Katharine Morrison McClinton

CHARLES SCRIBNER'S SONS · *new york*

B-2.67 [UJ]

THIS BOOK PUBLISHED SIMULTANEOUSLY IN
THE UNITED STATES OF AMERICA AND IN CANADA—
COPYRIGHT UNDER THE BERNE CONVENTION

PRINTED IN THE UNITED STATES OF AMERICA
Library of Congress Catalog Card Number 66-20461

ACKNOWLEDGMENTS

A number of friends and colleagues in Museums, Libraries, and Historical Societies have helped in locating material and photographs needed in the preparation of this book. Special thanks are due to Nancy O. Merrill, Curator of Glass, Chrysler Museum; Richard Carter Barret, Director-Curator, The Bennington Museum; Marvin D. Schwartz, Curator of Decorative Arts, The Brooklyn Museum; R. C. Morrell, Curator, and Muriel G. Harris, Librarian, The American Clock and Watch Museum; Bradley Smith, Ass. to the Director, Shelburne Museum; E. P. Hogan, Historical Research Librarian, The International Silver Co; S. Kirk Millspaugh, Vice-President, Samuel Kirk & Son; Ann Hogan, Gorham Mfg. Co; Janet Byrne, Ass. Curator, Print Dept., The Metropolitan Museum of Art; Amelia E. Mac Swiggan; Carolyn Scoon, Curator of Decorative Arts, Arthur Carlson, Curator of Maps and Prints, Shirley Beresford and the library staff of The New-York Historical Society; Elizabeth Usher and the library staff of The Metropolitan Museum of Art; also to the staff of the Art Reference Room of The New York Public Library, and the Reference Staff of the Welwood Murray Memorial Library, Palm Springs, California. A special thanks for photographs to the Index of American Design; Hallmark Cards Inc; The Old Print Shop; The H. V. Smith Museum of The Home Insurance Co; and to The Henry Ford Museum. To Carlton Brown, George O. Bird, and particularly to Gerald G. Gibson, Curator of Decorative Arts, and Katharine Hagler, Assistant, of The Henry Ford Museum, who gave so generously of their time.

TO MY FRIENDS AT
The Henry Ford Museum,

AND PARTICULARLY TO
THE EXECUTIVE DIRECTOR
Donald Shelley,
TO THE
CURATOR OF DECORATIVE ARTS
Gerald G. Gibson,
AND TO
Katharine Hagler, Assistant,
WITHOUT WHOSE CO-OPERATION
THIS BOOK COULD
NOT HAVE BEEN ILLUSTRATED

CONTENTS

7

8 · CONTENTS

COLLECTING AMERICAN VICTORIAN ANTIQUES

I. FURNITURE
(1840–1900)

THE dates for the Victorian period in America are approximate, for the style evolved gradually and the beginnings of the designs are seen at the end of the eighteenth century. Although the Victorian included many different styles used simultaneously, in each case the style was an interpretation of earlier styles and designs. It was an age of borrow and copy, and the American furniture maker and manufacturer, although he got a late start, excelled at the game. Indeed, Victorianism had its most successful blossoming in America, according to Rita Wellman in *Victoria Royal*.

Victorian furniture and Victorian design in general involved the use of motifs from the whole history of art. These motifs were revised and elaborated. Along with this look toward the past and the revivalism of older styles, there was the influence of industry in the mechanical innovations such as patented tilting chairs, automatic spring sofas, and beds that pulled out of bookcases. Industry also promoted the use of materials other than wood for the construction of furniture. The

Parlor from the Robert Milligan house, Saratoga Springs. Rococo styled carved furniture made by E. Galusha, Troy, N.Y. Carved marble mantel, carved gilt mirror. Crimson damask draperies hang from gilt cornices. The floral pattern carpet is crimson and gold. (*Brooklyn Museum*)

11

present-day popular iron, wire, tubular metal, and rattan furniture had their beginnings in the nineteenth century. Also such products as gutta percha and papier mâché were used by Victorian furniture makers. Comfort and usefulness were important factors in the design of such pieces as the ottoman and the Turkish overstuffed chair. The history of Victorian furniture in America is the history of a gradual change from individual craftsmanship in a small shop to mass production in the factory. Duncan Phyfe (d. 1854) employed as many as a hundred workmen although he himself directed the design of the furniture made in his shop, and Lambert Hitchcock (d. 1852) had started the shift to quantity production early in the century.

Although there were many different styles of Victorian furniture, there were only two major influences—French and English—and all the styles can be grouped under these major divisions plus the native American influence brought about by the taste, manners, and customs of rural America which produced the individual and original country Victorian. The French influence in American Victorian furniture is seen in the styles of Victorian Empire, Louis XIV, Louis XV, and Louis XVI and later in Art Nouveau. The influence is at first classic in the Empire, then rococo and baroque. The two woods used in making French-inspired American Victorian furniture were mahogany and rosewood, and later metal and exotic woods were used in Art Nouveau. The second influence to dominate American Victorian furniture was the English influence. This is seen in the Gothic, Renaissance, Elizabethan, and Eastlake furniture, and in the later Mission and Golden Oak which Grand Rapids made out of the Ruskin-William Morris efforts of reform. Country furniture was a simpler, less expensive popular expression, but it followed the influences of the more sophisticated pieces.

The first indications of the Victorian style in America were seen in the early 1830's. In the beginning the design influence was largely French. As the period opens we see a modification of the classic Greek forms of the French Empire Period. There is a similarity in structure, but the Victorian Empire is heavy and degenerate. Awkward, ungainly scrolls replace the round columns and claw and ball feet on tables, bureaus, and wardrobes. However, the workmanship and materials were generally good. Designs for this Late Empire furniture are shown in John Hall's book, *The Cabinet Maker's Assistant,* published in Baltimore in 1840. The book shows furniture with "C" and "S" scrolls for supports, legs and backs of sofas and chairs. These designs were intended for the use of the band saw, which had recently been invented, and carving was reduced to a minimum. Actual furniture of similar design is illustrated in the broadside of Joseph Meeks & Sons printed in New York in 1833. This style continued in popularity until the 1850's.

Alongside the classic forms was the use of historic ornaments of other periods, namely the Gothic, Elizabethan, and Renaissance; French Louis XIV, Louis XV and Louis XVI. The Gothic, although a favorite with Downing and the architects, was never used extensively in homes. Architects designed Gothic chairs for churches and public buildings. In the house Gothic furniture was thought suitable for the hall and library, but a few bedroom sets were also made and used.

The Louis XV style was the most important American Victorian furniture style. The outstanding maker of this type of furniture was Belter, who made furniture in his shop in New York City between 1844 and 1863. Similar furniture was also made by Charles Baudouine, M. A. Roux and Leon Marcotte in New York; George J. Henkels in Philadelphia, and A. Eliaers in Boston; Elijah Galusha in Troy, New York; S. J. Johns in Cincinnati, Ohio; and later in factories in Grand Rapids, Michigan and other large cities. This French rococo was especially popular in New Orleans and there were several cabinetmakers of French extraction working there, including Francis Seignouret, A. Seibrecht and Prudent Mallard, and later A. Debruille and Pierre Abadie. The Frenchman Anthony G. Quervelle was making furniture in Philadelphia from 1820 to 1856. The known pieces of his work show a combination of classic and Gothic motifs of design. As the interest in nineteenth century furniture increases the names of many more furniture makers and manufacturers will become known and much more furniture will be recognized and attributed to known makers in various parts of America.

The Gothic style developed early through the enthusiasm of the architects who themselves designed furniture. By the middle of the century the Renaissance style appeared in the exhibitions in London and Paris, and at the Philadelphia Centennial in 1876 the Eastlake style and the Turkish influence were the most dominant in the furniture exhibits. The majority of these exhibits were in bad taste. The furniture was covered with elaborate ornament mostly made by machine, and decorative motifs were used in indiscriminate combinations of various historical styles.

But there were tastemakers in the nineteenth century. The bad design and poor taste of the majority of the articles exhibited at the various World's Fairs from the Crystal Palace Exhibition in 1851 down to the Philadelphia Centennial, was criticized, especially by writers in the *Journal of Design* and the *Art Journal,* and efforts were made to improve the design. One of the best known reformers was John Ruskin and his writings did much to start the movement toward improvement. In America, the architect Andrew Jackson Downing criticized the taste of Americans and in his books sought to raise the level of the furnishings, especially of country houses, by suggesting the suitable decoration and styles of furniture. William Morris and his group of pre-Raphaelite painters contributed important suggestions but their work was never made for mass production. However, one of William Morris' followers, Charles Locke Eastlake, wrote *Hints on Household Taste* which went through many editions in England and reached America in 1872. Whatever Eastlake's good intentions may have been, his ideas and their adoption and commercialization by American manufacturers produced some of the worst examples of furniture design ever inflicted upon the American public. The fact that the American public embraced this bad taste and misuse of materials was due, to some extent, to the cheapness with which it could be manufactured, and so vast was the output that Eastlake was accepted in every home in America. The arts and crafts movement of Elbert Hubbard, the magazine *The Craftsman,* and the art of Louis Tiffany reached only a small audience. However, their efforts at improvement are recognized and admired today.

Parlor of Clinton Inn, Greenfield Village, Dearborn. Victorian Empire furniture. Argand lamp on table. (*The Henry Ford Museum*)

Victorian Empire (1840–50)

MUCH of this late Empire furniture was made by cabinetmakers who worked with hand tools, but although they continued to use earlier Empire forms, the furniture was heavier in style and ornamentation and had lost the most of its elegance of form. Metal decorative mounts as seen on the early Empire furniture of Duncan Phyfe and Charles

15

Honoré Lannuier were not used, and although Downing shows a chair with sphinx-carved front legs, such carving or animal legs are seldom to be seen. Victorian details such as machine-made wavy molding and applied flower and leaf carving replaced the finer details. This furniture has been ignored for years because it was inferior compared to the earlier Empire furniture. However, much of this furniture is of good workmanship. It is made of heavy mahogany or mahogany veneer over pine. Some pieces were made of rosewood and country pieces were made of maple, butternut, or other hard woods stained red or brown. This is furniture which is available for the average collector today, and while one may not want to assemble rooms full of examples, a few pieces can be used with good effect in the furnishings of any room and the prices are within the reach of the small pocketbook. This is the furniture that antique dealers scorned a few years ago. So far, few articles have been reproduced. The one drawback to Victorian Empire is chipped veneer which is expensive to replace. The collector should have certain information about the forms, the motifs of design, and the woods used. Since the chair is the piece most available and most popular, we begin our guide to collecting with the chair.

ABOVE. Victorian Empire mahogany ottoman with bracket feet. Similar ones made with "C" and "S" scroll feet. (*The Metropolitan Museum of Art*)

LEFT. Victorian Empire mahogany gondola side chair. (*The Henry Ford Museum*)

Victorian Empire *chairs* were of klismos type with concave back and curved saber legs. The open back of the side chair is "U" shape with the top rail arched in a flat curve, finger-molded, or crested with a carved leaf or flower and sometimes pierced with a central finger hole. The splat in the center of the back may be plain with finger-molded edge or serpentined with a carved center design; or sometimes the center splat is vertical vase-shaped or pierced with a cut-out design. A similar chair was made with cabriole legs. This type of chair was also made with rockers and there was an upholstered armchair with covered back and seat, open arms, and concave curved rear and front legs.

Victorian Empire *footstools* have "C" or "S" scroll legs and upholstered seats. Sometimes the cushion seat is upheld by a rectangular base with plain or serpentine skirt edged with plain or wavy molding, and has four bracket feet with casters.

Sofas have straight or serpentine backs, roll-over arms, and scroll, bulbous, or bracket feet. The front rail may be plain or serpentine with wavy machine molding. There is usually no carving, but the structure is outlined in ponderous bands and scrolls of pine veneered with plain and figured mahogany. The sofas are from five feet to six feet six inches in length, and the seat and back are fully upholstered, originally in haircloth. These sofas date from 1830 to 1855. A small armless love seat with scrolled or bracket feet is 40 to 44 inches long.

Victorian walnut couch with serpentine back and bracket feet. (*The Henry Ford Museum*)

Victorian Empire *tables* retain the lines of early Empire tables. The center tables and the folding-leaf card tables are supported by a bulbous pedestal or a lyre support that rests on a rectangular-shaped base with four scrolled feet. Sometimes these tables have flower and foliage carving, but more often there is no carving and the tops have a gentle serpentine curve. They are made of pine with mahogany veneer. Pedestal extension tables and circular or oval tilt-top tables of the Victorian Empire had a round pedestal with four cyma-curved feet. The pedestal of the extension table is hollow and contains a turned leg for support when the table is extended. These tables are made of rosewood, mahogany or black walnut. The tilt-top tables are often found in cherry or maple as well as mahogany and black walnut. There was also a rectangular drop-leaf table with four tapering turned legs which was made of black walnut or maple, or such fruit woods as cherry or butternut. This was made in the Middle West as well as on the East Coast from 1840 to 1865. A two-part dining table with each part supported by four legs and a center extension leg was made of black walnut, veneered mahogany, and maple, cherry or butternut. The legs are turned baluster-shaped or have bulbous fluted shafts.

BELOW. Victorian Empire mahogany pedestal table. (*The Henry Ford Museum*)

Empire cherry table. (*The Henry Ford Museum*)

The Victorian Empire *sideboard* often incorporates some of the finer details of earlier periods such as inlay panels, turned columns, and heavy claw feet together with wavy machine moldings. There is usually a rectangular backboard, plain or with a crest of carving, or it may be in the form of a broken arch ending in a carved rosette. Knobs are of stamped brass, wooden mushroom turned, or pressed glass. These sideboards were not factory made, but were usually made to order by a local cabinetmaker. Such sideboards are shown in the broadside of Joseph Meeks & Sons, New York cabinetmaker.

Victorian Empire mahogany card table with "S" scroll support. Mahogany chairs, rococo influence. (*The Henry Ford Museum*)

Square-top *sewing tables* with a baluster-turned or a plain tapering center shaft are supported by four scroll-cut legs.

The *desks* and *secretaries* of the Victorian Empire period are straight line with two or three drawers and a writing flap-shelf. The feet are bracket type or they may have short turned legs. They are made of mahogany veneer or native hard woods stained red.

The Victorian Empire *chest of drawers* began as a straight line piece but later incorporated the heavy cyma curve. Early in the period the chest had plain straight line construction with four tiers of drawers with mushroom-turned wooden knobs, bracket feet and a valanced skirt. The chest was made of mahogany, maple or black walnut, with drawer fronts veneered. Sometimes the top set of small drawers are recessed to the back of the bureau top. Often these chests have bulbous wooden legs and the corners are decorated in split-ball turnings. The drawers may be surrounded with wavy moldings or the top drawer may be ogee-molded. Some of these bureaus with two small side top drawers have round mirrors attached by a center base, or octagon mirrors attached by wooden knobs to a pair of "S" scrolls. Later these bureaus had heavy "S" scroll legs and feet extending down each side of the front.

The *bed* which matched these chests of drawers was the sleigh bed

Victorian Empire walnut bureau similar to one in John Hall's *Cabinet Maker's Assistant.* (*The Henry Ford Museum*)

made of veneer mahogany or rosewood, or pine or other soft woods painted. Head and foot boards were of equal height with curving top rails supported by flaring cyma-curved legs ending in heavy block feet. These beds are often smaller than average so that the standard modern box spring and mattress is too large and one must be made to order. When originally used the beds were usually set with the long side against the wall and a draped canopy was hung over both ends. Heavy beds with turned posts and head- and foot-boards of turned spindles were also made. A bed with massive turned posts ending in a heavy triangular finial and with a solid wood head- and foot-board was advertised in the *New York Directory* of 1840 as Gardiner's Premium Bedstead. The posts on later beds were shorter and had spool turnings. These were usually made of a combination of maple, birch, or pine, rather than mahogany, and date from 1840 to 1865. Empire *melodeons* and *pianos* were made in great quantities, according to the advertisements. The melodeons had lyre end supports and a scrollwork stretcher which upheld the lyre-shaped pedal support. The Victorian Empire spinet piano and early square piano has massive tapering octagon legs and heavy circular feet. The recessed pedal-frame is lyre-shaped. This piano is made of mahogany and rosewood veneer.

Victorian Empire sleigh bed, mahogany. (*Henry Francis du Pont Winterthur Museum*)

Victorian Baroque and Rococo (1840–1870's)

"MODERN French Furniture and especially that in the style of Louis Quatorze stands much higher in general estimation in this country than any other," says Downing in *The Architecture of Country Houses*. This furniture was really a combination of various French styles from Louis XIV to Louis XVI. All styles were made simultaneously, separately, and with mixed contours and details. It is impossible to separate them completely. At the beginning, the straight line baroque Louis XIV was favored. The chairs had straight baluster legs and a

Rosewood Victorian rococo parlor set. Carved mirrors and matching cornices. (*Campbell House Foundation, St. Louis, Missouri*)

high rectangular back with carved cresting. Elegant and expensive sets were made of rosewood, mahogany, and walnut. This furniture was made by cabinetmakers such as Meeks in New York and S. J. Johns of Cincinnati, who operated factories supplying furniture in great quantities. The ornate carving was often produced by separate carving factories. However, this furniture did not hold the popular eye for long. Instead, it was the rococo curves of the lighter Louis XV style that was demanded by the rising wealth of the middle class and this became the most popular French type. So much was manufactured that a great deal of this cabriole-leg Louis XV furniture with its elaborate scroll "C" and "S" curves and naturalistic carvings of fruit, flowers, foliage and birds exists for the collector today.

One of the remarkable developments in furniture production at this time was the creation of sets. There were sets of furniture for parlor, boudoir, bedroom and library as well as the dining room. French rococo was especially favored for the drawing room, and sets to be used there consisted of one or more sofas, a center table, an ottoman, an étagère, at least two arm chairs, and four side chairs. Downing names Alexander Roux and Platt of New York as the best known local makers, but there were many more including Leon Marcotte, who was listed in the New York directories from 1850, and who advertised furniture of "Black wood and gilt, Rosewood and satin, carved center tables, marble tops, marquetry." There were also makers in Boston, Newport, R.I., Rochester, Troy, Philadelphia, and as far west as Cincinnati, Ohio, and south to New Orleans.

Most of this furniture was made of rosewood, mahogany or walnut, but some was made of bird's-eye maple, chestnut, zebra and other woods. It was not only carved but often decorated with dull or matte-finished gilding. Cheaper sets were made of chestnut, oak or dyed maple.

While it is impossible to name all of the manufacturers of this rococo furniture, for they finally increased to the hundreds, there are a few who were working in the early 1850's whose ads give us definite information about the overlapping of styles and the furniture made in a specific year. In 1853 George Henkels of Philadelphia advertised

Victorian rococo walnut turned-spindle side chair.

Victorian rococo open-arm chair with floral carving. (*Carren Limited*)

Rococo walnut ladies' chair, 1850–1870. (*The Henry Ford Museum*)

Rococo carved rosewood chair. E. Galusha, Troy, N.Y. (*Munson-Williams-Proctor Institute*)

"Furniture in every style, Louis XIV, Louis XV, Elizabethan, and Antique with sculpture carving; ('called Renaissance in France but Antique in America,' says Samuel Sloan in *Sloan's Homestead Architecture,* Philadelphia, 1866) and Modern Style in Rosewood, Walnut, Mahogany, Satinwood and Maple." Henkel's shop burned in 1854, but he rebuilt and in the advertisement of 1857 he makes this interesting statement which probably was the reason for the shift of woods. "Walnut is now more used than all others. The supply of mahogany and rosewood is diminishing, maple has not met with much favor. Oak is in great favor for dining and library furniture." The ad which appears in Bigelow's *History of Mercantile and Manufacturing,* vol. XI, shows a cut of the shop with an extension table in the center. Henkel's rosewood furniture was elaborately carved "by the best European artists." It was usually upholstered in satin, and the tables, consoles and étagères had tops of "Siena marble." The furniture was not cheap.

Edwin Smallwood of Boston, in an ad of 1853, states that he

LEFT. Victorian rococo mahogany side chair with side cresting. RIGHT. One of the many variants of the Victorian rococo mahogany side chair. (*Both, The Henry Ford Museum*)

makes elegant sofas, tête-à-têtes, divans, arm and rocking chairs suitable for the southern and western market, together with "new style French lolling couches (chaise-longue) of elegant design constructed so they can be boxed in parts." Smallwood's furniture was made of mahogany, black walnut, and rosewood, and upholstered in Plush, Damask, and Brocatelle. W. & J. Allen of Philadelphia also advertised similar furniture in an atlas of 1856.

However, the best-known name associated with American Rococo furniture was John Henry Belter. Belter set up his shop in New York in 1844 about the time that Duncan Phyfe went out of business, and Belter soon took Phyfe's place as New York's most fashionable cabinet-maker. Belter's furniture was made of six to eight laminated layers of thin rosewood. The wood of the outside layer runs vertically. The backs of his chairs were made from a single concave panel and were almost completely covered with carving. Crestings on sofas, mirrors and

LEFT, TOP AND BOTTOM. Rosewood carved-back parlor chairs. John Belter. (*The Metropolitan Museum of Art*)

BELOW, LEFT. Rosewood carved rococo side chair attributed to Belter. (*The Henry Ford Museum*) RIGHT. Rosewood parlor chair attributed to Belter. (*Carren Limited*)

aprons of tables are also intricately carved with grapes, leaves, roses and scrolls of interlacing foliage. Belter's furniture combines delicacy and strength. In the beginning some chair backs were covered with interlacing scrolls. The carving was elaborate and finely executed. The scroll-back chair had an arched cresting. A simple side chair had an upholstered back with smooth flowing scrolls and a small carved cresting at the top of the back.

The chairs most often associated with Belter have balloon-shaped backs framed by a scroll that is arched and topped by a carved crest. The scrolled medallion in the center of the back has a carving of leaves and a center bunch of grapes enclosed in the scrolls. The seat has a bow-front with a carved flower at the center. The front legs are cabriole and the back legs plain and tapering. Some side chairs have taller backs and the carving includes several bunches of grapes and leaves, with a cresting of roses at the top of the chair back and roses at the knees of the scrolled cabriole legs. Sometimes the side chair has an upholstered oval in the back which is surrounded by scrolls enclosing wide borders of elaborate rose or grape carving. There are also armchairs with intricate scrolls of grape and leaf carving set around a center medallion of upholstery and crested with a large carved rose.

Rosewood rococo sofa pierced and carved with flower, cornucopia and acorn design. (*The Metropolitan Museum of Art*)

There were also lady chairs without arms, but with high balloon-shaped or oval backs surrounded by carving. Belter sofas were made with triple-arch backs of one-piece construction with a continuous band of naturalistic carving enclosed in "C" scrolls, with crests at each end and in the center. There are also carved bosses or roses on the knees of the short cabriole legs and at the center of the front seat rail. Some sofas have a graduated asymmetrical arched back, tall at one end and lower at the other end. There are also couches with one end left backless.

Belter tables had an oval or cartouche-shaped top usually covered with marble. This was upheld by four cabriole legs which were supported by a carved X-shaped stretcher holding a center urn-shaped vase of carved flowers. The apron of the table was of openwork carving

Laminated carved rosewood table with marble top. John Belter. Stuffed birds under glass dome. (*The Henry Ford Museum*)

Rosewood card table made by Charles A. Baudouine. (*Munson-Williams-Proctor Institute*)

of roses, grapes, and foliage. Toward the end, Belter's carving became more naturalistic and on such pieces as the rosewood bed in the Brooklyn Museum the carving is made up of leaves and connecting vines. The legs on later furniture became heavier and straighter. Belter's furniture was covered by patents but few pieces were signed.

George Henkels of Philadelphia and Charles A. Baudouine of New York also made laminated rosewood furniture as well as the more common, less expensive type of French carved furniture. The furniture in President Lincoln's bedroom at the White House is of Belter type. The oval table has a wide apron of grape carving and the tall headboard of the bed is crested with elaborate openwork carving. The maker of this furniture is not known. French rococo furniture was made in many parts of America by many cabinetmakers and manufacturers. Some was well made and hand-carved, but much of it was cheaply made by machine.

The typical Louis XV rococo chair of the period was balloon-backed with plain finger-molding and with or without a carved crest at the top of the back or on the serpentine splat in the open back. The carving was of grapes, a pear or plum, with leafage; or on more elaborate chairs, a rose. These chairs have cabriole front legs. They are usually made of black walnut, but some are also made in rosewood. There is also an upholstered balloon-back side chair and gentlemen's and ladies' balloon-back upholstered armchairs. Open-arm upholstered chairs have a rectangular back topped with a bit of flower or fruit carving and there is also a similar chair with rockers. These were made in walnut, mahogany, or rosewood and were originally upholstered in black haircloth. The heavy Sleepy Hollow lounge chair was completely upholstered within a finger-molded mahogany frame.

The rococo sofa was made in various forms. The one with a serpentine back and enclosed arms is the most common. It is made

LEFT. Mahogany rocker with black haircloth seat. BELOW, LEFT. Rococo walnut side chair with balloon back and paired "C" scroll splat. RIGHT: Balloon-back mahogany side chair with finger-grooved carving and foliated tendrils. (*The Henry Ford Museum*)

Common-type mahogany settee with carved foliated tendrils and haircloth upholstery. Similar sofas made in walnut. Matching mahogany side chair. (*The Henry Ford Museum*)

with finger-molding, in walnut, and in mahogany and rosewood with carved cresting at top sides and center. Similar sofas were also made with open arms. There were also serpentine-back sofas with an oval medallion of upholstery in their back and some have triple-backs resembling three oval-backed chairs attached together. There were also side chairs and armchairs with upholstered oval backs, and all had cabriole legs. Along with these rococo chairs and sofas there would be an oval table with cabriole legs and a center vase stretcher, or an oval table with scalloped apron and a center pedestal supported by four legs, an elaborately carved étagère, or a tall pier glass with a low elaborately carved table at its base. This would be set between windows whose cornices were often carved to match the pier glass and its table. Closely connected with the popular Louis XV rococo was the heavier straight line Louis XIV style with its broken pediments and baroque cartouche crests on tall rectangular-backed chairs. The Louis XVI style was also copied, but where it was a light delicate style in France, in America it became heavy and bawdy.

Meeks' Cabinet and Furniture Warehouse,
No. 699 BROADWAY, and 333 and 335 Fourth Street.

New and elegant Designs, of superior Workmanship, at reasonable prices, manufactured of the very best well-seasoned and selected material, under the supervision of the firm, whose reputation has been established seventy years. Every description of Furniture manufactured to order and executed promptly.
Goods packed and shipped to all parts of the world.

Renaissance Revival parlor sofa and chairs. Meeks' Cabinet and Furniture Warehouse. (*Harper's Weekly*, November 14, 1863)

The Renaissance Revival Style

THE Renaissance Revival style with its heavy straight lines and architectural ornament such as pediments, cartouches, and applied medallions of carved decoration came into prominence at the Crystal Palace exhibitions. At the New York Crystal Palace Exhibition in 1853 Thomas Brooks of Brooklyn exhibited a large carved rosewood buffet; a carved sideboard of Renaissance design with carved panels of game and fish was also exhibited by Rochefort. A similar sideboard has a center panel scene of dogs and game and side panels of fish and lobster, while a hunter with bow and arrow stands within the broken pediment at the top of the sideboard. This was made by E. W. Hutchins of New York. Alexander Roux also exhibited a carved walnut sideboard and table. A sideboard of more restrained design by Daniel Pabst of Philadelphia was made c. 1870 and is now in the Philadelphia Museum of Art. A beautiful cabinet of rosewood with tulip and ebony inlay panels within

32

its heavy Renaissance architectural structure lines is in the Newark Museum. It was made by Leon Marcotte of New York in the 1870's.

A great deal of Renaissance Revival furniture was also made at Grand Rapids at about this date. The heavy sideboards have panelled bases with rounding ends which have doors and drawers which conform to the rounded shape, and each panel has a spray of carved fruit. This is surmounted by one or more shelves with pediment and carving. These large sideboards were usually made of black walnut or mahogany in quality furniture factories such as Berkey & Gay in the 1870's. Large round extension tables with center ornate pedestal were made to match. There were also smaller round Renaissance marble-topped tables with a pedestal consisting of a turned column and four scroll legs. A smaller marble-topped table with similar column support and scroll legs was used as a lamp or vase stand. There was also a rectangular

Walnut Sideboard, Renaissance style, Daniel Pabst, 1869. (*Philadelphia Museum of Art*)

Renaissance Revival walnut side chairs with burl walnut panels. (*The Henry Ford Museum*)

Renaissance Revival armchair with incised and carved ornament from Congress Hotel, Saratoga Springs. (*Carren, Ltd.*)

table supported by scrolled trestles and a turned stretcher. It has carved flower and leaf medallions on the drawer and table ends. This table was factory-made in black walnut. A Renaissance Revival drop-leaf table with trestle end supports was also made in black walnut. The upholstered Renaissance Revival armchair has heavy turned legs or legs accented with round medallions, fluted columns, and was often decorated with black enamel and gilt. There is a matching side chair. The Renaissance Revival bed was made of black walnut with panels of burl veneer. The headboard is tall and massive. It is divided into architectural panels and topped with a pediment centered by a large cartouche. The footboard is one of similar design with curved ends. The matching bureau has three drawers with leaf-carved wooden handles or tear-drop pulls, a marble top, and a mirror with bracket shelves and a pedimented scroll top. Sometimes there are small drawers at the base of the mirror, and sometimes the top drawer becomes two side drawers and there is an open space in the center and the huge

Renaissance Revival table with Corinthian column legs and vase on stretcher. Leon Marcotte. (*The Metropolitan Museum of Art*)

ABOVE. Renaissance Revival walnut chest with foliated handles and split urn applied decoration. Mass produced. RIGHT. Renaissance Revival walnut bureau. BELOW. Renaissance Revival bed, oak with walnut trim and burl maple panel. (*The Henry Ford Museum*)

mirror extends to this level. A simpler version is made with four drawers and a curved top mirror supported by scrolls. A heavy tall black walnut secretary of rectangular construction with glass doors above a lower desk is seldom carved except for rosette details on the lower doors and at the top of the glass doors. Renaissance Revival furniture is so large and heavy that there is no place for it except in the old high-ceiling mansion, few of which exist today. However, where such articles as the bed and chests of drawers are well constructed and can be bought cheaply, they may be cut down to smaller pieces of furniture.

Renaissance Revival walnut secretary desk with broken pediment and foliated carving. 1865–1875. (*The Henry Ford Museum*)

Milligan Study from Saratoga. Gothic Revival chairs and Gothic influence in corner étagère, panels on secretary-bookcase, and details of lamp base. (*Brooklyn Museum*)

Victorian Gothic (1840–1865)

GOTHIC style furniture was favored by Andrew Jackson Downing. In his *Architecture of Country Houses* he includes a lengthy discussion of Gothic, and gives the characteristic details and illustrations of the Gothic furniture available in America in 1850. An antique settle for a

38

large hall in country style is made of oak or walnut with a leather cushion. A hall stand and cottage chairs with rush bottoms or haircloth seats, armchairs with Gothic arches and pieced work, and book cases with Gothic panels in their glass doors all show taste and simplicity. Similar chairs with a combination of classic outline and Gothic detail are illustrated in Edgar G. Miller's *American Antique Furniture* and there is a similar chair made of mahogany with pointed arches and trefoil in the Brooklyn Museum. Downing also illustrates more elaborate Gothic furniture—armchairs with twisted turnings, partly Elizabethan; a day bed, a round center table and dining room sideboard. All these are made of oak and are ornate and heavy with elaborate carving of pointed arches, crockets, and trefoil piercing. These were made by Roux of New York and in a footnote Downing says: "The most correct Gothic furniture that we have yet seen executed in this country is by Burns and Tranque, Broadway, New York. Some excellent specimens may also be seen at Roux's." Gothic details were also used in the country furniture made by Hennessey of Boston, and by John Jelliff of Newark, New Jersey.

Although Gothic furniture has been thought of as church furniture a great deal of it was made for private houses. Just how much exists today is questionable since it was long ago relegated to the attic or the bonfire. In addition to that made in quantity by furniture manufacturers, individual pieces and sets were made by such architects as William Strickland, Charles Notman, Thomas U. Walter, and A. J. Davis in the 1830–40's. Some of this furniture exists today, especially in the old houses in and near Burlington, New Jersey, and in St. Mary's Episcopal School in Burlington; in several old New York churches and parsonages; and undoubtedly there is much undocumented Victorian Gothic scattered throughout America since many old furniture ads picture Gothic chairs.

A. J. Davis was probably the most active designer of Gothic furniture and his diaries show that he was sketching and designing furniture as early as 1828. He not only designed chairs, tables, pulpits and organs for churches, but for the many houses which he built along the Hudson and in upper New York State and Connecticut. Although the Davis designs were original he studied Loudon's *Encyclopedia of Architecture* and Pugin's *Gothic Furniture,* which were among the books in his library.

In 1836–38 Davis was designing a Gothic house for Nathan Warren at Mt. Ida, Troy, New York. At the suggestion of the client, Davis drew sketches. According to notes left by Davis' son, two Gothic armchairs, a library sofa and an organ case were designed by Davis and made for Nathan Warren.

In the 1840's Davis also designed the furniture for the J. Angier Gothic cottage in Medford, Mass., and for the Joel Rathbone mansion, Kenwood, near Albany. On May 31, 1844, the entry in his *Diary* at the New York Public Library reads: "Mr. Rathbone here. Designed a table for him." He also designed a "Gate lodge and furniture," and in 1846 "Rathbone Details Bookcase." The sketch of the drawing room at Kenwood in Downing's *Country Houses* shows a Gothic mantel and Gothic chairs, settee and tables, and also an Elizabethan armchair.

A bill to J. J. Herrick dated September, 1853, indicates that Davis had the following Gothic furniture made for Herrick:

> 8 small armchairs with crockets and back, Gothic
> 8 lady chairs to match
> 1 table for dining room extension and round

Victorian Gothic washstand, cottage type. Mahogany veneer on pine. (*The Henry Ford Museum*)

In 1838 Davis began work on a Gothic mansion for the Pauldings in Tarrytown. In the *Diaries* there are many references to this house, which, with its Davis-designed furnishings, stands today as a monument to Davis' ability and an example of the best work of the era. Between June and September, 1841, Davis sketched "50 designs for furniture for Paulding—$50.00# (*Diary,* Metropolitan Museum of Art). In the *Diary* in the New York Public Library is this item of September I, 1841: "At Tarrytown 6 days and sketching for furniture (Paulding). October 5, 1841: "Designing furniture for Paulding. Oct. 5, 6, 7, 8—Nov. 6. Returned to Pauldings. Designs for furniture." *Diary,* Metropolitan Museum of Art, page 364: "Met P. at Dobbs Ferry. Rode to Wrights', Astounding furniture." In a note added to the *Diary* in the New York

ABOVE. Walnut side chair with carved back showing rococo and Gothic influence. (*The Henry Ford Museum*)

RIGHT. Rosewood chair with open quatrefoil and carved crocket finial. John Jelliff. (*Newark Museum*)

Public Library we are told: "Richard Byrnes of White Plains made with Wright cabinet work at Pauldings."

The opening of Lyndhurst, which was originally the Paulding house in Tarrytown, New York, and the discovery of many pieces of Davis furniture stored there for many years, brings our attention to Davis as a furniture designer. The chair from Davis' own home, probably Kerri cottage, is simple in design and the workmanship is excellent. It is made of rosewood and was given by Davis' son to the Museum of the City of New York.

Picture gallery at Lyndhurst, showing Gothic paneling and Gothic side chairs designed by A. J. Davis. (*Collection, Avery Library, Columbia University*)

Country couple sitting in fancy chairs; table, painted wood graining. Water color by Joseph H. Davis. (*The New-York Historical Society*)

Victorian Country Furniture (1840–1900)

FROM the standpoint of the collector today, Victorian Country Furniture is the most important of all Victorian designs because it fits into the present-day house and is available and inexpensive. In the vocabulary of this writer, Country Furniture includes all furniture of simple design made of less expensive woods such as pine, hickory, maple, chestnut, walnut and other native woods. Country Furniture is often reminiscent of older styles. Actual pieces include Windsor, Hitchcock, and other fancy chairs, spool furniture and cottage furniture. Country Furniture is not a separate style, but a simpler presentation of other styles. It reflects the more sophisticated furniture which was being made at the same time. What we now call Country Furniture was originally called Cottage Furniture, and included spool furniture and cottage French style. At first it reflected the Empire style, later it became related to Louis XV, and some Country Furniture goes back to early American inspiration.

Generally, however, Country Furniture was based on the needs and requirements of middle class customers in the rural districts rather than those of people in the large cities. Practicality was the keynote for Country Furniture. There were no ornate sideboards or heavy-headed beds or large padded chairs. Instead there were essential pieces of furniture such as dry sinks, washstands, light side chairs, and sturdy but small beds, tables, and chests of drawers. There is little carving or decoration and the furniture was usually painted instead of oiled or varnished. This furniture was made in large quantities by rural furniture makers and carpenters, and later mass-produced in factories throughout America. There are great quantities of it today and it can be found in all parts of the country at reasonable prices.

Country-style washstand and bureau. Pine, painted and grained. (*The Henry Ford Museum*)

Early Country Furniture varied with the locality. Thus the Country Furniture of New England, the furniture of the Shakers, and the Pennsylvania Dutch furniture, as well as that made in the Middle West, all had their own distinguishing characteristics, but by the time we reach the middle of the nineteenth century there were factories turning out Country Furniture and shipping it to all parts of America and the regional differences disappeared in the mass production. Early ladder-back chairs and small hickory rockers with rush seats, trestle and tavern tables or drop-leaf tables of maple or ash originally made for the kitchen are all popular country pieces today. The cherry

LEFT, TOP AND BOTTOM. Walnut chest of drawers with towel rack. Country piece with Renaissance Revival influence. Country-type pine washstand. 1850–1880.
(*The Henry Ford Museum*)

BELOW. Kitchen table. Walnut frame stained dark brown. Top unfinished ash boards. c. 1850.
(*The Index of American Design*)

cupboard on a table with turned legs, the storekeeper's desk, the schoolteacher's slant-top desk and even the pupils' desk supported by cast iron, are dear to the heart of the Country Furniture enthusiast. Maple commodes with marble tops and carved-leaf drawer handles were made after 1850. There are also Eastlake walnut commodes with brown marble tops and metal drawer pulls. These were made in the 1880's, but today they are stripped of varnish and sold as *Country Furniture*. Washstands, kitchen safes and dry sinks, kitchen tables, and even the dentist's golden oak cabinet are other pieces that are now collected.

In writing about Victorian Country Furniture it is a mistake to omit slat-back, banister-back and Windsor chairs, or Hitchcock and fancy chairs, for although they were originally made in the eighteenth

Late nineteenth century dry sink and cabinet, pine, with Gothic panels in doors. Pennsylvania. (*The Index of American Design*)

century, they continued to be made with slight variations in the Victorian nineteenth century. Late types of these chairs are found in the average shop today and are our earliest pieces of nineteenth century Victorian Country Furniture. Early chair makers advertised themselves as "Fancy and Windsor Chairmakers." By 1825 almost every town had such a chairmaker. Besides their use in private homes fancy chairs were used on steamboats, and in hotel lobbies. As late as the 1840's fancy chairs were used in great numbers in Castle Garden, New York, and in 1850 Windsor settees were made for church pews and for use in schools.

Windsor chairs were made in factories from 1850. The Windsor chair is an all-wood chair. Its back is made of spindles joined to a conforming saddle seat. The legs are turned with vase or bamboo turnings. Various woods are used: poplar for the seats, hickory for spindles and arms, and hickory, ash, maple, or other light woods for legs and stretchers. Old Windsors were always painted, mostly green but also red, black, yellow, or white. Windsor chairs are classified according to the shape of their backs. There are the fan-back, loop-back, sack-back and comb-back. There was also the low-back or horseshoe Windsor armchair of which the Captain's Chair is a variant. Victorian Windsor types were made as late as 1870 and 1890. These include hoop-backs, square-back Windsor side chairs, and a variety of Windsor loop-back which were made in factories and sold as kitchen chairs. There was also a low-back Windsor with caned seat and carving and a hand-hole in the center of the back which was made of oak or ash for use as a dining room chair. An office chair similar to a Captain's Chair was mass-produced in hickory and oak. These are the Windsors seen today in shops all over the country.

Hitchcock started the making of fancy chairs in quantity and the same type chairs were made at many factories throughout New England in the middle of the nineteenth century. The Hitchcock factory closed in 1852, but in 1949 reproductions of Hitchcock chairs began to be made at the old factory in Riverton, Connecticut. The typical Hitchcock chair was a combination of Directoire and Sheraton. It had a rectangular back with one or more horizontal splats, a turned top rail, with a center pillow, slender turned legs, and a rush or cane seat. Later seats were made of wood. The chairs were painted red-brown or black to imitate wood. Stencil decoration of gold was applied to the legs and splats and the top rail was stenciled with a design of fruit or flowers in a bowl, basket or cornucopia. Designs of roses, shells, a lyre or an eagle were less common. The chairs that concern the collector of Victorian furniture would be made after 1840. If they are marked they would be stenciled "Lambert Hitchcock, Unionville, Conn.," but few of them are found marked. The chairs of late Hitchcock type are usually made by other makers. Some have rush or cane seats and others have wooden seats and the back slats may be horizontal or upright arrow-shaped. Sometimes the chairs are painted yellow instead of reddish-brown and often late stenciling is of a landscape, or a scene showing a country seat may be hand-painted as on the Maryland type fancy chair. There were good stencil painters of the old type working in Maine and Massachusetts until the end of the century and any chairs stenciled by them would be well done. A late fancy chair has a crested balloon-back with three turned spindles, a cane seat, and

LEFT. Painted pine comb-back Windsor chair, 1870. (*The Index of American Design*) CENTER. Painted and grained maple side chair with caned seat, 1860–1875. (*The Henry Ford Museum*) RIGHT. Maple side chair with turned legs and caned seat, 1860–1875. (*The Henry Ford Museum*)

turned legs. Fancy chairs were usually made for the dining room but were also used in the living room, bedroom, and on the veranda. Fancy and painted chairs were popular until the 1890's and many late ones that were made for kitchens are collected for the drawing rooms of today.

The Country Furniture of the nineteenth century was known as Cottage Furniture. *Godey's Lady's Book* was illustrating this Cottage Furniture from 1849 and Downing in his *Architecture of Country Houses,* 1850, recommends Hennessey of Boston, who made Cottage Furniture and supplied orders from various parts of the Union and West Indies. Downing describes it thus: "This furniture is remarkable for its combination of lightness and strength. It is very highly finished and is usually painted drab, white, gray, a delicate lilac, or a fine blue—the surface polished and hard, like enamel. Some of the better sets have groups of flowers or other designs painted upon them." The illustrations of bedroom sets include sleigh beds and bureaus, washstands and a wardrobe which show the influence of French Empire, but the tables, chairs, and towel racks have spool turnings. These sets could be pur-

LEFT. Hitchcock chair painted black with stencil design in gold and colors, 1832–1840. (*The Index of American Design*) CENTER. Hickory rawhide-bottom ladderback country chair. Witte Memorial Museum. (*The Index of American Design*) RIGHT. Late Windsor armchair. Pine and maple, painted green with red line trim. "Firehouse" type. (*The Henry Ford Museum*)

chased with or without "gilt lines" or marble tops. Horace Farrington of New York (1848–1860) illustrated more elaborate cottage furniture —"French style, enameled and grained." At the New York Crystal Palace Exhibition in 1853 enamelled and ornamental Cottage Furniture was exhibited by Gillies & Byrne of New York and by Hart, Ware & Co., of Philadelphia. By 1856 Joseph Meeks was advertising Cottage Furniture, and an interesting letter now in the New-York Historical Society, written in 1859 by the furniture manufacturer J. W. Mason of New York, to his client in Danbury gives added information about Cottage Furniture. He says: 'The seats are made of white wood, arms like Boston Rockers in imitation Rosewood, Black Walnut, Oak, Maple and drab or green color, the price being the same for either color. Drab color we think the best for halls unless it is desirable to match some other color on account of the walls of the house."

This type of furniture continued to be made in Massachusetts, Vermont, Maine, Ohio, and by the Sheboygan Chair Co. in 1890.

Spool furniture forms another group of Country Furniture. Spool furniture is turned on a lathe. It was made in small shops at the beginning of the nineteenth century and later mass produced in factories. The turnings were in various forms; spool, button, knob, sausage, bobbin, vase and ring. Spool furniture represents a resurgence of

Jenny Lind type cherry spool-turned bed, 1850–1870. (*The Henry Ford Museum*)

the turned Flemish furniture of the seventeenth century. However, Victorian spool furniture which was made from 1840 was influenced by the Elizabethan according to Downing, who illustrates two of Hennessey of Boston's bedroom sets made for the bracketed cottage. The simplest set shows a spool bed with vertical spindles in the head- and footboard and a washstand, dressing table, oval mirror and a side chair, all with some form of twisted or spool-turned leg. They were made of black walnut, maple, or birch. The more elaborate set has heavier ball turnings and could be had in dark wood or painted drab "enriched by well-executed vignettes in the panels." There were also spool beds with posts and head and foot boards made of plain wood instead of spindles. Sometimes a pediment topped the row of spindles.

The later style of spool bed had curved corners, and was called a Jenny Lind bed. There are also high-posted spool beds and spool cribs and cradles. There were Pembroke and oval drop-leaf tables with spool-turned legs. Small rectangular side tables and serving tables, washstands and dressing tables also had spool-turned legs. They were made of black walnut in the factory, or of maple, poplar, or cherry stained or painted. There were also towel racks and tall shaving stands, stools and chairs made with twisted or spool legs. Split spindles were applied to the sides of chests of drawers and the frames of mirrors. Spool furniture was the first factory mass-produced furniture. It was simple in design and inexpensive in price.

LEFT. Cherry spool-turned table, 1850–1865. (*The Henry Ford Museum*) RIGHT. Walnut towel rack, 1860–1880. (*The Henry Ford Museum*)

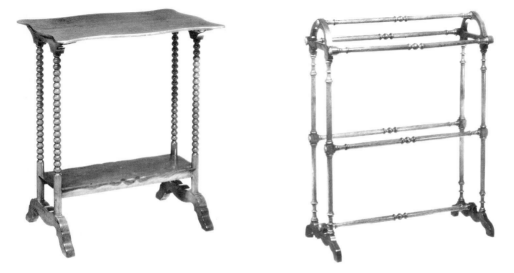

Today the various types of spool beds are easily found. Those of natural wood are more expensive because of the job of removing the sometimes many layers of paint. Towel racks and small tables are also inexpensive, but washstands are more in demand and thus more expensive. The most sought after piece is the small sewing or bedside table, especially when made of maple, cherry, or mahogany.

Another type of Country Furniture which is in demand today and therefore expensive, is the simple *Shaker furniture*. The restraint and

LEFT: Mahogany dressing mirror with twisted supports; Elizabethan style. BELOW LEFT. Walnut side chair with twisted supports and turned legs; Elizabethan style. (*The Henry Ford Museum*) RIGHT. Carved oak settee; Elizabethan-medieval style. (*Mr. and Mrs. William Crawford*)

integrity of their religious life is reflected in stark simplicity and purity of form of this furniture. The severe beauty is due to fine proportions of line and mass and a harmonious relationship between the parts, which result in artistic unity. Shaker furniture has no decoration and little turning. The legs of chairs and tables are thin and tapering and the chair backs have simple slats; one or two on the low dining room chairs and three on side chairs, while the backs of the rocking chairs had three or four slats and often a narrow rod across the top. Armchairs had mushroom knobs at the end of the arms. There were arm rockers and small armless sewing chairs. The seats of the early chairs were made of rush, later seats were of woven tape. Much of the Shaker furniture

Group of Shaker furniture made before 1850. Round stand, pine with curved molded maple feet. Small spool stand. Wall rack with Shaker bonnet hanging. Shaker rocker with scrolled arms and turned pointed finials. (*Celeste and Edward Koster*)

Early nineteenth century Shaker drop-leaf table and side chair. Hancock Museum, Massachusetts. (*Celeste and Edward Koster*)

was made of pine, but apple, cherry, maple, and pear woods were also used. The early furniture was painted or stained red.

The Shakers made several different types of tables. A long trestle table had square or rectangular supports with flat or curved shoes. There were pine ironing tables with crossed braces and horizontal stretchers. Drop-leaf tables were made with a drawer and with or without a rectangular stretcher supporting base. There were also small oval tables, sewing tables, and round and square tripod stands. The long kitchen table had two drawers, a shelf beneath and end supports. A bread-cutting table had a rim around three sides of its top and a drawer. It stood on four tapered legs.

Pennsylvania Dutch painted chair with one arrow splat in back, c. 1850.
(*The Index of American Design*)

Early Shaker chest showing Chippendale influence in the base and top moulding.
(*Celeste and Edward Koster*)

The Shaker case-furniture included chests, blanket chests, chests of drawers, high chests with many drawers, cupboards, washstands, and writing desks. Beds were made of maple and pine with a low-posted head and footboard. The narrow cots were painted green. Both beds and cots were set on rollers. In 1874 and 1876 the Shakers of New Lebanon, Columbia County, New York, issued illustrated catalogues of chairs, foot benches, etc. R. W. Wagan & Co. also issued a catalogue. The later commercial Shaker furniture can be recognized by the changes in design and workmanship.

The Rocking Chair

THE rocking chair is an American invention and an American institution. It was a particular favorite of the Victorian furniture makers. Slat-back, banister-back, ladder-back and Windsor rocking chairs with rush seats go back to the middle of the eighteenth century, but the majority of the existing antique rocking chairs have rockers that were added. Chairs were not made with rockers until 1800 and the rocking chair did not really become popular until after 1840. Windsor rocking chairs were made both with oval and square backs and there are comb-back and fan-back Windsor rockers. Some early rocking chairs show Empire influence in the shape of their top rails and the center vase-like splat in their backs. With the advent of the fancy chair the rocker gained in popularity and both Windsor and Sheraton fancy chairs were made with rockers.

The famous Boston rocker developed from the Windsor rocker. Both the Windsor rocker and the Boston rocker have a solid wooden

LEFT. Mahogany rocker with rococo carving and black haircloth upholstery, 1860–1875. (*The Henry Ford Museum*) RIGHT. Curly maple rocker with birdseye maple crested rail and cane back and seat, 1850–1860. (*The Henry Ford Museum*)

seat and thin spindles in the back and a top rail, but where the top rail of the Windsor rocker is usually more delicate and has a narrow fan or a comb-back top rail, the Boston rocker has a large top rail and the pine wooden seat curves up at the back and down in the front. These curved sections are separate pieces attached to the seat. The legs and arms were usually made of maple, the spokes and rockers of ash and the top rails of pine. The Boston rocker is more decorative than the Windsor. The designs include not only fruit and flowers, but the Boston rocker is often decorated with painted seascapes or landscape scenes. Sometimes the scene is historic, such as the Harrison Log Cabin and Cider Scene which was painted on the rocker during the campaign of 1840. Boston rockers were made in many forms and many variations. There were small rockers made without arms and there were children's rockers. William Eaton of Boston decorated rockers until the end of the century and often labeled them "Boston Rockers—W. P. Eaton." Some rockers are also marked "M. L. Gates, Boston."

The Pennsylvania Dutch rocker had a back splat instead of spindles

LEFT. Boston rocker with painted and stencilled decoration and typical rolling crest and curved seat. (*The Henry Ford Museum*) RIGHT. Shaker rocker with tape back and seat, mushroom knobs at ends of arms and turned finials. (*The New-York Historical Society*)

and both the top piece and the splat were painted with typical Pennsylvania Dutch designs of bright red and yellow tulips, daisies, or birds. It was made of maple and other hard woods. The Shaker rocking chairs have tall backs with three slats and a woven, shaved wood seat. The spindle supports of the chair are simple with no decorative turning. A Windsor rocker of maple with pine seat is called a "Burlington" or "Shelburne" rocker. This type was later painted black with floral decoration on the top splat.

There are many other types of later country rockers with rectangular or oval backs framed in maple, and with backs and seats of cane. These rockers are found both with and without arms. They often have a carved flower or fruit motif or a spray of hand-painted flowers. They are made of walnut, maple, or birch. In 1853 the Oswego Chair Factory manufactured "Grecian cane rockers" as well as Boston rockers, and in 1859 a Reception Rocking Chair, that stood on casters and rocked, was patented by Terry & Wills of New York. There were also Eastlake rockers on platforms, and small folding rockers upholstered in carpet tapestry were made late in the century.

LEFT. Late nineteenth century maple Shaker rocker made at Mt. Morris, New York. (*The New-York Historical Society*) RIGHT. Late Victorian rocking chair with turned construction. Maple painted black with yellow trim. Berlin work upholstery. (*The Henry Ford Museum*)

Eastlake (1870–90)

ONE wonders what would have been the result and what type of furniture we would be collecting today had Whistler's beautiful Peacock Room, which he decorated in 1872, been exhibited at the Centennial instead of Eastlake's cabinets. But Eastlake's book, *Hints on Household Taste,* had reached America in 1872 and, instead of Whistler's Peacock Room, examples of Eastlake's sturdy oak furniture were exhibited at the Centennial in Philadelphia in 1876. The book had already created the market for this furniture and there was an immediate demand for Eastlake. Grand Rapids complied with the public's desire. In his book, Eastlake championed honest craftsmanship and a close alliance between the materials of which an object was made and its design. He wrote: "The natural grain of such woods as oak, rosewood, and walnut, etc., is in itself an ornamental feature. But where an effect of greater richness is aimed at, two legitimate modes of decoration are available for wood, viz. carving and marquetry or inlaid work." Fine examples of furniture are shown as illustrations in the book, but the Grand Rapids interpretation relied on the mass production of machines rather than the personal expression of the craftsman.

The fundamental outlines of the furniture which Eastlake advocated were complied with, and the furniture was made with a straight line rectangular structure, but the quality of workmanship was shoddy and the design motifs of machine incised and veneer panels which were glued on obliterated the simple rectangular structure, and Eastlake's original ideas were completely misinterpreted.

Eastlake furniture was made of many different woods, but that which we see is mostly oak or walnut. It was decorated with machine scroll carving and burl walnut veneer panels. The carving consisted of jigsaw scrolls and rosettes and incised lines of geometric design. Sometimes the furniture was painted black with gold linings. Tables and chests had marble tops and the hardware escutcheons and handles were oxidized or plated brass. The marble for the tops of Eastlake furniture was imported and there were many kinds available, including Carrara, Siena, Egyptian, Brocatelle, Levante, Pyrenees, Bardella and Lisbon.

The typical Eastlake side chair is of straight line construction. It has turned tapering front legs and front stretchers with ring turning. The seat is caned and the open back has three horizontal crossbars divided by turned spindles, two on the lower tiers and a row of from four to six at the top. Sometimes the top rail has a panel of burl veneer. Another style of Eastlake side chair has a machine-cut vase splat in its back. The back and seat are joined together by machine-scroll arms and the seat is caned. These chairs were sold in sets and included a small rocking chair of similar design with a caned seat and back. Eastlake office chairs had the same spindle decoration in their backs. They were set on a steel screw which allowed the chair to tilt back and forth. This was upheld by four bracket feet. An Eastlake chair with upholstered seat and back was set on a similar center screw with four leg supports and was used as a desk chair or a piano stool. There were also rectangular upholstered piano stools without backs.

Eastlake chairs, custom-made of exotic wood. Carved panel designs show Renaissance influence. (*Mr. and Mrs. William Crawford*)

The typical Eastlake parlor chair has a back and seat upholstered in black horsehair. The frame is oak or walnut with applied panels of burl veneer and there is a rosette in the center of the back rail. Three of these chair backs were joined to form a settee. An armchair of ebonized wood made for the Rockefeller House at 4 West 54th Street, New York, in 1885, is now in the Brooklyn Museum. Although it shows Turkish influence in its elaborate embroidered and fringed upholstery, the panel in its back contains a row of spindles similar to those in the panel at the top of the cheap Eastlake side chairs.

The Eastlake platform rocker was a rectangular upholstered chair with arm rests and open arms. It sat on a platform of jigsaw scrolls and the chair and base were connected by springs which allowed the chair to rock. These chairs were made of walnut or oak and were sometimes a part of the parlor set. They were called Queen Anne Patent Rockers. They were also made with a bamboo-turned frame. An Eastlake Windsor was advertised in 1870. This was an armchair with a finger

Eastlake sofa, walnut, with Renaissance vase in center of back. (*The Henry Ford Museum*)

hole in the back rail and these chairs were for offices, hotels, and public institutions. But the bête noir of all Eastlake chairs was the folding chair with carpet seat and back. It was trimmed with wide fringe which hung down over the front of the seat. These chairs were advertised by Heywood Bros. of Gardiner, Massachusetts, in 1883–84. The *tête-à-tête* or conversation chair which had first been made earlier in the century was also in popular favor now. It was built on an "O G" structure holding two chairs with upholstered seats and backs made up of spindles. The padded top rail was hung with long fringe. These chairs were often placed in the center of a room.

Eastlake tables were rectangular or square with marble tops and aprons decorated with typical applied rectangular panels of burl veneer, and machine-carved rosettes. Some table tops were upheld by bracket legs and a center stretcher, others had four legs or tripod supports. There were several types of *desks* and *secretaries* made for both women and men in Eastlake style. The Eastlake ladies' desk has small drawers in the side of its tall base, a flap-top writing compartment and a shelf upheld by spindles and topped with a row of spindles and a pediment. It is made of oak with burl walnut veneer panels. A hanging wall desk has side shelves for bric-a-brac and opens to reveal a desk with drawers, pigeonholes and a fold-down flap for writing. This desk was patented in 1887. There is also a tall Eastlake bookcase secretary with cabinets below the slant-top desk with a glass-doored cabinet above for books. This is topped by an oval fan pediment of machine carving or by a panel of burl-veneer. Similar secretaries and smaller desks were also made with cylinder fronts. The Eastlake sideboard was made of walnut or a combination of walnut and maple. It is much taller than it is wide. The lower chest of drawers is topped with several shelves backed by mirrors and upheld by scroll-cut brackets and surmounted by a rectangular pediment. Similar shelves to hold bric-a-brac were built around the mirror above the mantel. Sometimes this mantel, shelf, and mirror construction was sold in one piece—"ash mantel and mirror." There is also a tall Eastlake bookcase with a set of drawers below the double glass doors. It has an overhanging top with a gallery of scrolled brackets.

The *Eastlake panelled bed* was usually made of oak or walnut. Less expensive beds were of lighter woods such as birch, maple, or ash. Eastlake bedroom sets were advertised in the following combinations: "Silver maple and mahogany, bamboo and maple, whitewood ornamented and ash." Beds five feet wide were advertised for southern trade. The tall headboard and the lower footboard were divided into rectangular panels of burl veneer or incised line decoration. They had an overhanging cornice or the headboard may have had a rectangular, triangular, or fan-shaped pediment. The bedroom set also included a

LEFT. Eastlake fall-front desk, walnut with burl walnut panels. c. 1880. (*Grand Rapids Public Museum*) RIGHT. Eastlake hall stand with inlaid panels, gouged carving and row of spindles in cresting. (*Grand Rapids Public Museum*)

Eastlake bedroom set with incised lines and Renaissance influence in rectangular cresting. (*The Henry Ford Museum*)

tall *wardrobe,* and a *bureau* or chest with three ample drawers and a large rectangular mirror surmounted by a pediment of scrolls and machine-cut brackets. The mirror is also fastened to the chest with brackets. The top of the bureau is covered with marble and sometimes there are small drawers at either end. There are also tall sets of drawers for gentlemen, which have five or six drawers. These are decorated with incised line designs and have a gallery of turned spindles at the top. There are tall *Eastlake mirrors* and *pier glasses* with oak or walnut frames decorated with panels of veneer or ebony gilded with geometric line patterns. They are crested with a rectangular pediment. Corner whatnots, hanging shelves and wall brackets of jigsaw oak or

Eastlake pump organ with gouged carving, inlaid panel and rows of spindles. Esty Organ Co.; c. 1900. (*Grand Rapids Public Museum*)

walnut scroll work added to the maze of scroll and jigsaw and incised line machine decoration that characterizes the Eastlake period.

When one recalls the beautiful William Morris designs for chintz and wallpaper and some of the rooms in England which were decorated by Morris and also by Eastlake it seems a sacrilege to call this American factory furniture "Eastlake." Yet Eastlake it is and for lack of anything better people are buying it today not as collector's pieces, but for use. Bad as this furniture is, it is not any worse than some of the hybrid designs still being manufactured and foisted off on the average American housewife who has little feeling for good design. Eastlake is strong if not well made and the pieces found in second-hand shops are usually in good condition, cheap in price, and need little repair.

Other Types

At the same time that America was furnishing with Eastlake there were several other types of furniture which came into being. There was an increased interest in *overstuffed* furniture probably due not only to the American's love of comfort, but to the international attention which was directed toward Turkey and things Eastern. Every house had its *Turkish cozy corner,* piled high with sofa cushions, and the *ottoman* and overstuffed chairs reached a zenith of popularity.

Overstuffed chair, Turkish influence. Tip-top papier mâché table inlaid with mother-of-pearl.
(*The Henry Ford Museum*)

Victorian fancy chair with bamboo turnings.
1840–1880. (*Index of American Design*)

ABOVE. Bamboo-turned screen with Berlin
work tapestry. Brass standing lamp. 1890.
(*The Henry Ford Museum*)

LEFT. Maple table painted black, marble top.
Eastlake with Oriental influence in carved
panels. (*The Henry Ford Museum*)

BELOW. Walnut tête-à-tête, Turkish influence.
1880–1900. (*The Henry Ford Museum*)

Whatnots, Étagères and Hanging Shelves

No Victorian parlor was considered properly furnished unless it had a whatnot or étagère for the display of bric-a-brac and curiosities. All the collected odd pieces of china, shells, coral, bits of carved ivory, and family pictures on fancy standing frames found a resting place on the shelves of the whatnot or étagère. The simple whatnot is really a country piece and thousands of these were made, while the étagère, derived from the French, is a larger, more sophisticated piece of furniture designed for the parlor of the more affluent citizen. The whatnot usually had five shelves of graduating size—small toward the top. The shelves were joined and supported by spool-turned posts of various patterns or by machine-cut bracket supports. There were usually fancy openwork

LEFT. Victorian walnut étagère with Renaissance Revival cresting. Gothic and Rococo influence in mirror framework. (*The Henry Ford Museum*) CENTER. Victorian walnut five-shelf corner whatnot. (*The Henry Ford Museum*) RIGHT. Eastlake étagère. Mahogany with typical fan and ball motifs and grooved line carving. (*Carren, Ltd.*)

galleries at the back of the shelves and the fronts of the shelves were serpentined or cyma-curved. There were corner whatnots with triangular shelves and rectangular and square whatnots to set flat against the wall. Whatnots were usually factory-made of black walnut. Finer examples were made in mahogany or rosewood, and cheaper ones were of assorted woods stained to look like walnut. Some whatnots were made with drawers or with a cupboard base below the shelves. These were also usually made of walnut, but were made by cabinetmakers as well as in factories and are less numerous and more expensive than the ordinary corner or rectangular wall whatnots.

The étagère was really a glorified whatnot. However, it was not made as a corner piece but as a wall piece—for parlor or hall. The shelves of the étagère were usually built at the sides of a mirror. The base or stand with two shelves surmounted by a mirror had tiers of small shelves on either side and a carved crested top, varying with the style of furniture it was made to match. Thus the Louis XV étagère has a carving of flowers or grapes while the Renaissance style étagère has an architectural pediment with vase or cartouche, and the Eastlake étagère has a fan or square-crested pediment. The tall pier-glass étagère was surrounded by tiers of shelves and attached to a low marble-topped table. These were, of course, more expensive pieces and were made of rosewood as well as black walnut with veneer trim. An étagère with a cupboard base had open shelves in its curved sides and a mirror with rows of shelves on either side and a heavy crested pediment. There was also a late Eastlake hanging étagère form with center rectangular mirror and intricate flower and bird carving interspersed with shelves.

Small hanging shelves with scroll-cut brackets were made by novelty manufacturers who also made wall pockets, picture frames, and towel racks. These were called jigsaw or Sorrento carving and were cut out of thin wood by machine and decorated with cut-out leaves, birds, and heads of animals such as fox or deer. There were also small corner shelf brackets of carved leaves and branches. These were made in three parts, the back pieces hinged and folded and the triangular shelf fitted between and hooked to one side piece to hold it

LEFT. Hanging corner wall shelf, cherry. 1860–1880. RIGHT: Hanging walnut wall shelf, scroll-cut design. (*The Henry Ford Museum*)

in place. Many of these small hanging shelves were made by home craftsmen. Information and designs had been available since the Centennial where a demonstration booth had given impetus to this kind of handiwork. Sometimes the wall pockets had Berlin work or beaded pockets.

Various Materials

THE Victorian Age was also noted for the use of materials other than wood. Iron, brass, and later, wire furniture was used in conservatories and as porch and garden furniture. Iron furniture was introduced in the middle of the century but it gained its popularity in the 1870's. Iron furniture was made for use in both house and garden. American iron furniture was cast in parts and assembled. For indoors there were plant stands, cabriole-legged tables, mirror frames, hall racks and umbrella stands and beds. Pieces for indoors were painted black with gilding or

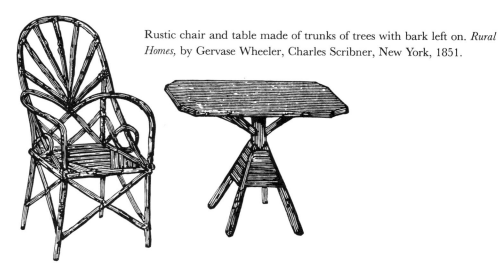

Rustic chair and table made of trunks of trees with bark left on. *Rural Homes,* by Gervase Wheeler, Charles Scribner, New York, 1851.

in colors imitating wood. They were rococo in form and decoration. The round center table usually had a marble top, a scrolled and pierced skirt and an ornate pedestal leg or ornately scrolled cabriole legs braced with a stretcher. The cast iron bed had a foot- and headboard of ornate scrolls and leaves. There were also cast iron washstands and towel racks. In 1853 the Rochester Novelty Company put out a catalogue advertising japanned and bronzed iron piano stools, umbrella stands, foot scrapers, and store stools, and in 1856 the Berlin Iron Company advertised tables, chairs, beds, washstands, hall racks, stools, umbrella stands, sewing baskets and frames. Dozens of other iron companies throughout America were making iron furniture, mirror frames, and iron cases for clocks. The mirrors had small rectangular frames of flower and leaf scrolls, or an eagle design, or had supports of crinolined ladies with cupids above and a flag attached to the center stand. These were made for ladies' dressing tables and the latter type were called Jenny Lind mirrors. Iron furniture for the garden included settees, benches, tables and chairs. These were made in designs of grapes and leaves, ferns, lily of the valley, and all-over scroll pattern. The grape design with a scrolled leaf cabriole leg was the most common and these have been reproduced today. Some of this furniture was also made in a rustic design of tree branches. Furniture of rustic wood had been made earlier in the century and Downing had advocated its use and described it, first in his book, *Cottage Residences,* and later, in the magazine, *The Horticulturist.* There are also sketches of rustic furniture designed by A. J. Davis.

In the Crystal Palace Exhibition in London in 1851 rustic furniture was exhibited by the Oneida Community, and rustic furniture

BELOW AND ABOVE. Cast iron Gothic settee, marble-top table, hall chair, umbrella rack. *A New Phase in the Iron Manufacture.* New York, 1857. (*The Metropolitan Museum of Art*)

was made by James King in New Haven, Connecticut, in 1860. Wire chairs "for lawns, cottages and piazzas" and wire folding hall, office and rocking chairs were advertised by the New York Wire Railing Co. in their catalogue of 1857. They also picture folding iron beds in "scroll and diamond pattern, high post gothic, lyre, Harp and Union pattern all-over" as well as wire and "swinging gothic cribs." Any of these beds if found today would not only be decorative for use in the present-day house, but valuable as well.

Wicker and bamboo furniture were also popular at the end of the century. The wicker furniture was made in fancy scroll designs and seems to have been related to Eastlake. Gothic designs were also made. The bamboo furniture has an oriental derivation. There were settees, hall racks, tables and bookcases in this stained bamboo which are now coming into the shops. *Bentwood furniture* which originated in Austria was imported from Vienna, but it was also made by several American furniture companies. J. W. Mason advertised Bentwood chairs in 1870 and the Sheboygan Chair Company was making American Bentwood in 1890. This Bentwood furniture was made of birch. *Animal-horn furniture* is another novelty made at the end of the century which has found its way to the antique and secondhand shops and is collected. Chairs and tables had their backs, legs and arms made of steer or buffalo horns

Rattan settee and chair, Chinese design made by Berrian & Co., New York City. c. 1850 *Rural Homes* by Gervase Wheeler, Charles Scribner, 1851.

and the seats were upholstered in leather. In 1889 Robert S. Gould of New York City advertised "Plush and fur hassocks with polished horn legs." The upholstery was of goat or sheep skins or plush and it was trimmed with silk cordings, or a fancy brass apron was tacked on. This horn-legged furniture is considered the height of sophistication with collectors today. Papier mâché furniture which had been made in America and exhibited by American companies at the Crystal Palace in London in 1851 also continued in popularity.

Papier Mâché

ANY discussion of Victorian furniture should include papier mâché, since no parlor of the early Victorian era was complete without at least one table, chair, or writing case of papier mâché.

The French invented papier mâché, but it was also made in England as early as 1772. The base of papier mâché was a damp mixture of vegetable matters, paper, hemp, etc., which was pressed into sheets upon an iron mold. Several such layers were pressed and pasted and finally dried in an oven before being taken from the mold. The article was then waterproofed and the shiny varnish coats applied. Then the piece was ready for the final decoration which was to give it real interest and value. Motifs of decoration included flowers, birds, butterflies, Chinese and English scenes, Gothic architectural scenes and geometric patterns. Methods of decoration, beside regular painting, included bronze put on in powdered form with swabs instead of brushes, mother-of-pearl inlay, and real or artificial gems set in tinsel and arranged in a pattern under glass.

Articles made in papier mâché include trays, fans, screens, tea caddies, writing cases, blotter covers, paper and book racks, bellows, inkstands, jewelry boxes, sewing boxes, snuff boxes, card cases, buttons, tiptop tables, tea tables, chairs and cabinets.

Papier mâché was made at Birmingham, England, by Jennens & Bettridge from 1816 to 1864. Another center was at Wolverhampton where Walton & Company made a specialty of tea trays.

Papier mâché was also made in America by several companies who exhibited at the New York Crystal Palace in 1851. Evans and Millward of New York exhibited a work table and a music stand and Ward & Company also exhibited several small pieces of furniture. In 1853, Bowler, Tileston & Co. of Boston made papier mâché frames, mirrors, work boxes, and cabinet work. But the only company that left any record of making papier mâché was the Litchfield Mfg. Co. (1850–1854), of Litchfield, Conn. The principal output of the Litchfield Mfg. Co. was papier mâché clock cases which they furnished to Jerome & Co. and other Connecticut clock dealers. The most elaborate case was the "Navy, 8 day Timepiece," illustrated in Jerome & Co.'s catalogue of 1852. It was a wall clock in the form of a shield, crested with a spread eagle, flags, and cannon. The Kossuth, an eight-day striking clock, was illustrated in the same catalogue. It also had a papier mâché case. It was decorated with mother-of-pearl inlay and had a center medallion with a picture of Kossuth.

Although the papier mâché clock case was probably the staple which kept the company going, they also made small tip-top tables, standing screens, hand screens, sewing stands, sewing boxes, album covers, and daguerreotype cases.

Papier Mâché sewing stand. Pierced fire screen. Litchfield Manufacturing Co., 1850–1854. Litchfield Museum. (*Shirley S. De Voe*)

Papier mâché snuff boxes were also made with American scenes and portraits of American presidents. In the mid-century there were snuff boxes with engraved portraits of Polk, William Henry Harrison, and Zachary Taylor. However, the boxes themselves were probably made in England.

In choosing papier mâché the collector should select his pieces for aesthetic values, for the painting and decoration determine the worth of the piece. Good pearl inlay is placed so that the grain of each piece in a flower or leaf reflects the same color. Even small snuff boxes often have fine painted portraits or scenes.

From the middle of the century there were also many mechanical inventions which produced furniture that tilted, rocked or reclined to increase the comfort of the occupant. There was also an interest in furniture that folded and converted or was made to serve several purposes. Lindley's Patent Bedstead had been exhibited at the American Institute as early as 1843. In 1848 A. J. Davis records the armchair which was given him by the cabinetmaker Burns. "Mr. Burns presented me with a revolving armchair, carved round back, claw legs, and covered with plush worth $30.00." In the Crystal Palace Exhibition in London in 1851, the American Chair Company of New York exhibited a patented iron-spring chair which attracted considerable attention. A reclining chair that folded out as a bed, Hobe's patented extension table, and a revolving chair patented by M. W. King & Co. of New York were also exhibited. In 1855 M. W. King advertised an Invalid's parlor armchair. This was Louis XV style and was set on four cabriole legs attached to a center pedestal. Also a combination firescreen and desk was made by Victorian cabinetmakers of rosewook or mahogany veneer. It had curved bracket-feet with a turned stretcher between. An armchair which converted into a child's crib, folding beds which could be stored in a small space, and the sofa bed, were all invented and produced in the latter half of the nineteenth century. The advertisement of Nathaniel H. Van Winkle of New York stated that he had the largest variety of combination furniture in the world owning and controlling 30 different patents for sofas and lounge chairs.

Raspberries, Cake and Ice Cream, oil on canvas by C. P. Ream (see Dessert No. IV, page 120)
Harnett signature is forged. (*Collection of Oliver E. Jennings*)

II. DECORATIVE
ACCESSORIES

Clocks

A CLOCK consists of two parts—the case and the inward mechanism or works. The age of a clock may be quickly judged by the cabinet work of the case, by its dial, and by the decoration on the glass, but it takes years of study to be familiar with the clock mechanism. For this reason, and since the average clock collector is interested in the appearance rather than the mechanism of a clock, the clock is considered as furniture in this chapter. Indeed, when it is said that a clock was made by a certain clockmaker it is understood that he only made the works. The case was always made by a cabinetmaker, the dial by a dial maker, the hands by a metal worker, the engraving or painting by an engraver or painter. However, the clock works controlled the form and appearance of the clock and the case was usually made to fit the clock. Also, it is the mechanism which is the certain index to the date, and the value of a clock. Names of clockmakers are recorded, but we know little about the cabinetmakers who made the cases or the various other craftsmen employed to finish and decorate a clock.

77

For the antique collector mainly interested in clock cases, there are three classifications determined by the position the clock occupies; namely, the floor or grandfather, the wall, and the shelf clock. Wall clocks included wag-on-the-wall, banjo, and lyre clocks. The majority of floor, tall-case or grandfather clocks were made between 1770 and 1840 and there were not enough made after 1840 to include them here. However, some tall clocks were made, and you can find late tall Victorian clocks with mahogany or walnut cases or in weathered oak mission cases or even fancy wicker cases. The banjo clocks were also early, patented by Simon Willard in 1802. However, a late type banjo was made after 1842 by Howard & Co. of Boston with circular or rectangular bottom and rounded sides.

Lyre clocks which were related to the banjo clock were made by Aaron Willard, Jr., and several other companies in the 1840's and 1850's. The case of the lyre clock was made of mahogany and carved with acanthus leaves; under the face is a door with decorated glass panel. Lyre clocks are rare and expensive. The well-known pillar and scroll mantel clock with its scroll top, pillars, scrolled skirt, bracket feet and painted scene on the glass was first made by Eli Terry in about 1820. The pillar and scroll was also made by other Connecticut, New England, and Pennsylvania clockmakers. Terry style mantel clocks with wooden works were cheap as compared with the more elegant Willard clocks

TOP, LEFT. Mahogany veneer banjo clock, c. 1850. Maker unknown. (*Mr. & Mrs. William Vernon Ashley II*) LEFT. Mahogany veneer clock. H. Welton & Co., c. 1843. CENTER. Black painted and stencilled case with mother-of-pearl inlay. c. 1850. J. C. Brown Manufacturer. RIGHT. OG frame clock with painted tablet. 1859–1861. Burwell & Carter. (*Bristol Clock & Watch Museum*)

and whether made by Eli Terry, Seth Thomas or other makers they were the favorite clocks of the average household until about 1840. Gradually less graceful forms evolved with heavier side columns, less flowing scroll tops, and a flat base with carved animal claw feet, ball feet, or flat bottoms without feet. These are often decorated with a stencil or have a carved and gilded eagle on their tops. Some of these clocks had flat tops and had the appearance of an Empire mirror. Eventually the pillar and scroll clock was replaced by the Looking Glass clock of Chauncey Jerome which had a large looking glass on the face under the dial. Later a third panel with decorations was added and the position of the mirror changed.

In about 1840 the popular OG clock appeared. It was made in six or more sizes. The wave-like OG molding is veneered and is identical with that of the mirrors of the period. The lower part of the glass of these clocks was decorated with such scenes as the Merchants Exchange, Philadelphia, or Monticello, home of Jefferson. Clocks with OG cases were made by Seth Thomas, E. N. Welch, and the New Haven Clock Company down into the 1890's. Now that the case maker no longer had to design the clock case to hold the vertical fall of the weights, he could introduce new designs according to his own whims.

About 1845 the Gothic steeple and the Beehive appeared. The Gothic steeples followed the furniture trend of the day. Some steeples

TOP RIGHT. Mahogany and rosewood sharp Gothic case. c. 1864. E. N. Welch. RIGHT. Double steeple Gothic case. c. 1845. Birge & Fuller. LEFT. Cornice top, columns and scroll supports. c. 1850. Forestville Mfg. Co. CENTER. Round Oriental Gothic ripple case with lyre design on frosted glass panel. c. 1850. Brewster & Ingrahams. (*Bristol Clock & Watch Museum*)

LEFT. Beehive clock case, rosewood veneer. c. 1850. Brewster & Ingrahams. CENTER. Venetian-type rosewood case. c. 1870. E. Ingraham & Co. RIGHT. Black lacquer case with mother-of-pearl inlay. c. 1850. C. Jerome. (*All clocks on page Bristol Clock & Watch Museum*)

were pointed and others had many turnings. The door frames of the better clocks were brass and the door had a brass knob, while the lower part of the glass was either engraved or painted. Some clocks had double steeples and the cases were often ripple-framed. The Gothic case was designed by Elias Ingraham, but this clock was copied by all Connecticut clock makers and remained popular for many years. Rounded top, octagon top, and Beehive were other popular shelf clock styles. These clocks were made in mahogany and rosewood or combinations of the two and often the wood casing is rippled. Another common type of the 1840's–1850's was a plain rectangular veneered wood case with a crudely painted panel below the clock dial.

After 1837 when brass works replaced wooden works the number of clocks increased, and in 1852 the catalogue of Jerome & Co. advertised clocks suitable for Public Buildings, Churches, Banks, Stores, Ships,

LEFT. Cottage case of rosewood veneer. 1831–1855. J. C. Brown.
RIGHT. Cottage-type case with stencil decoration. c. 1850. C. Jerome.

Steamboats, Railroad cars, Parlors, Halls, and Kitchens. Clock cases were also made of many different materials such as marble, bronze, china, glass, zebra wood, iron and papier mâché decorated with pearl inlay, handpainting and stencil. The styles of clocks continued to relate to furniture styles and even the names of clocks reveal the current interests of the times. In the Jerome & Co. catalogue of 1852 the rococo influence is particularly noticeable, not only in the shape of the clock cases, but also in the materials and decoration.

Especially popular were clocks with papier mâché cases. These clock cases were made by the Litchfield Manufacturing Co. and supplied to clock makers, including Jerome & Co. who put in the works. The cases made by the Litchfield Manufacturing Company include a large "Oriental Mantel" with a scene in the cartouche panel below the dial, a Navy eight-day clock with eagle, flags and cannon, a small Tom Thumb, and a Kossuth with a portrait of Kossuth below the dial. The papier mâché cases were decorated with stencils, hand painting, and mother-of-pearl inlay. This was the only firm that made papier mâché cases, but similar cases were made in lacquer and cast iron painted and inlaid with mother-of-pearl by J. C. Brown; Terry, Downs & Co.; E. & A. Ingraham; Bradley Mfg. Company; Otis, Upson Clock Company; and Ansonia. The cases were also made in OG and Cottage shapes as well as the fancy rococo forms. An iron case resembling

LEFT. Cast iron case with gold and mother-of-pearl inlay. c. 1853. E. & A. Ingraham. CENTER. Papier mâché case with gilt and mother of pearl. c. 1855. Litchfield Mfg. Co. RIGHT. Cast iron case with embossed leaves and birds and mother-of-pearl decoration. c. 1860. Bradley Mfg. Co. (*Bristol Clock & Watch Museum*)

a Gothic cathedral with Gothic fretwork painted decoration and two towers was made in several sizes and distributed by the American Clock Company, New York, in the 1860's. These iron clocks were made between 1850 and 1870.

In 1869 Bronze Clock Cases were introduced to compete with the French bronze clocks which were so popular as mantel decoration. The cases were cast in Connecticut and the movements were made by Connecticut clock makers. A design called "Amor" was made up of rococo curves and topped by a cupid with bow and arrow. Other cases had horses, lions, or human figures as crests, and cases showed both Grecian and Egyptian as well as Oriental influence. There were also cases with popular designs such as the sailor with anchor, a baseball clock, and comical Blinking Eye clocks. In 1885 H. H. Tammen of Denver, Colorado, advertised novelty clocks including shapes of an anchor, a cross, a horseshoe, a star, castle, miner's cabin, and artist's palette. These forms were studded with quartz rock crystal and other semi-precious gems. It is not known what company supplied the clock works but William L. Gilbert of Winsted, Connecticut, made clocks in the form of an anchor and a cross in 1879, and George B. Owen made a clock in the form of an artist's easel at about the same date.

In the 1880's carved and scrolled kitchen clocks were made of oak and walnut by E. N. Welch and E. Ingraham. Some of these scroll clock

LEFT. Pressed oak kitchen clock. c. 1900. E. Ingraham Co. CENTER. Carved scrolled kitchen clock. Renaissance influence. c. 1880. E. N. Welch. RIGHT. Black marble case with gold leaf decoration. c. 1890. Waterbury Clock Co. (*Bristol Clock & Watch Museum*)

cases are fantastic beyond description, but others are comparatively interesting. The glass was decorated with a stamped design and often had the company monogram. Jigsaw clock cases with Seth Thomas movements were also sold, complete with movement and pattern for making. Also in the 1890's, black marble mantel clocks with gold leaf decoration and with gilded figures on their tops were popular. These could be purchased with or without the figures. The 1881 catalogue of E. Ingraham & Co. showed clocks of enameled metal with gilt and bronze ornaments and decorated panels. The bronze top and side ornaments could be purchased separately. These included eagles, vases, a seated figure of Ceres, and figures of cavaliers. A toilet table clock had a dial on one side and a mirror on the other. Some clock cases were made of mosaic or marbleized rosewood. Small bedroom or mantel clocks of Dresden, Delft, and Haviland china decorated with painted flowers were also popular in the 1890's. The cases were usually imported, but several American companies, including Willets of New Jersey, made flower-decorated clock cases of Belleek porcelain. Clock cases were also made of pressed glass in the Daisy and Button design, in milk glass and in cut glass.

The value of a clock is determined by the established identity of the maker, either by the printed sheet with his name pasted to the inside of the case or by having the works identified by an expert. The

LEFT. Decorated china clock case. c. 1890. New Haven Clock Co. CENTER. Rosewood veneer case, "Patti", Renaissance design. c. 1895. Welch, Spring & Co. RIGHT. Renaissance Revival design shelf clock. c. 1875. (*Anonymous*). (*Other clocks, American Clock & Watch Museum, Bristol, Conn.*)

age cannot be determined except within the years that the maker was in business and the clocks that he was known to make at a certain period. If the clock is not running be sure to have it checked by a repair man before you buy it. He may also be able to identify the maker. From the standpoint of the average collector who wants a clock as decoration the condition of the case is important. Is the wood in good condition? If veneered, is the veneer chipped? Is the painted glass panel in good condition? Is it original or has it been replaced? Glass panels on old clocks were etched, later they were printed from blocks. Designs include a wreath or heart of leaves, a lyre, eagle, or flowers. Painted panels also vary in workmanship, some are hand-painted and some are stenciled. And finally, which should be firstly, is the clock of pleasing design and does it fit in with your decorative scheme?

Mirrors and Picture Frames

VICTORIAN mirrors and picture frames are given very little attention in most books because they are not fine antiques. In both design and workmanship they are inferior to the mirror frames of earlier periods. Victorian, like other period mirror frames and picture frames, follow the style of furniture in design and general characteristics. There were large ornately carved frames for the more formal Victorian style rooms and rustic frames for the cottage. Many mirrors continued to be made in two sections of glass, but later they were made of one piece of mirror glass. A bevelled edge is a sign of a late date.

Victorian Empire Mirrors, which are the first included within our Victorian boundaries, were larger and heavier than those of the early Empire period. The most popular type still showed the influence of the Sheraton mirror. It was made with two sections of glass and the upper section usually contained a painted emblem such as the eagle or a flower piece or landscape. The most interesting of these had the *Constitution* or the *Guerrière* or "Perry's Victory." These mirrors have cornices under which was a row of balls and there are columns on each side of the glass. On this type of Victorian Empire mirror the delicate

carving has disappeared and the columns are carved in rings. These mirrors are usually gilded, but a popular form had gilded ring sections interspersed with longer sausage-shaped sections of dark stained "ebonized" wood. Sometimes these frames are of walnut or mahogany without the pediment top. These have square corner blocks. A similar mirror with pilasters on all four sides and square corner blocks centered with rosettes is known as a Tabernacle Mirror. Thousands of these were made in the 1840–50's. Mirrors of both of these types were made in three sections for overmantels. These were Victorian copies of earlier mirrors.

Still other mirrors are framed in a wide gold frame with borders of reeding. These mirrors were made by expert craftsmen, by village carpenters, and also manufactured in small looking glass factories. Most of the inexpensive ones were made in rural districts and the workmanship is crude, being cut with carpenter's planes. The painting in the panels is amateurish folk painting. It consisted of village scenes, a church, a landscape or a country couple. Since these mirrors were usually gilded or gilded and painted the wood is not important.

Another type of Victorian Empire mirror had a single panel of glass held in a rectangular "OG" frame of mahogany veneer. Some of these mirrors were pine covered with gesso and gilt, sometimes they were made of light wood or of black lacquer and gilt. Later some were made of oak or walnut. These mirrors were made in several sizes and could be hung either vertically or horizontally. Such mirrors are available in shops today but many have chipped veneer and this is not easily repaired. However, it is possible to remove the veneer and refinish the pine frame for use with Country Furniture. Another type of country mirror had a simple molded rectangular frame with rounded corners. It was pine covered with gesso and painted to imitate wood or enamelled in light colors to match the painted cottage bedroom sets. Later these mirrors were made of black walnut; some carved with tree branches and crested with

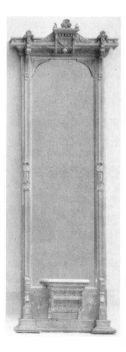

TOP. Empire mirror. Black and gilt frame. Painting of cottage scene in upper panel. c. 1840. (*The Henry Ford Museum*) BOTTOM. Pier glass with marble console framed with pilasters and cornice with shell finial. (*The Metropolitan Museum of Art*)

leaves were made in the 1860–70's. There were also octagonal mahogany veneer mirrors originally made to sit between the scroll supports on the mahogany veneer bureaus. Oval mahogany veneer mirrors had rounding narrow frames.

More ornate mirrors were made to accompany more formal Victorian styles. There were oval wall mirrors, large crested overmantel mirrors usually of broad rectangular shape, and tall pier glasses which reached to the ceiling. These frames are usually pine covered with gesso and gold leaf or painted to imitate rosewood. The oval mirror was the popular shape. There were oval mirrors with a simple convex frame, but most of the mirrors had a crested gesso decoration of fruit and flowers. The same manufacturer who made mirrors also made window cornices and picture frames and a whole ensemble could be had to match. In 1840 John Doggett & Co. of New York City advertised looking glasses, and Richards Kingsland advertised matching looking glasses and cornices in 1855. Both square and oval elaborately decorated mirrors are shown in the advertisements of looking glass manufacturers of the 1850's. The gesso carving on these mirrors consisted of leaves, fruit, flowers, and interlacing "C" and "S" rococo curves and pierced borders of round openings. These mirrors and frames relate to the rococo Louis XV furniture. A dressing table ensemble of an oval mirror with a flower-carved crest flanked by figures of naked children holding baskets of fruit with candles was made in about 1855. Pier and console mirrors elaborately decorated with foliage, fruit and birds richly gilded were also made in the 1850–60's. The gilded overmantel mirror has a rectangular frame with an oval crested top heavy with gilded gesso carving of fruit, and flower gilded mirrors are often found with parts of the composition flowers or scrolls broken or missing. Such a frame can be regilded, but the proper job with gold leaf and burnishing and the replacement of composition parts can be quite expensive.

Many of the larger Eastlake mirrors were made of walnut. There were simple rectangular walnut framed mirrors of several sizes and table mirrors with a straight or oval top. The Eastlake pier glass had an architectural flat pedimented top with a center cartouche. The sides and top of the mirror are ornamented with incised geometric line designs and panels of burl veneer. There were also mirrors with cast iron frames made to hang on the wall and small oval dressing table mirrors with ornate flower and scroll designs and sometimes an eagle crest. These were set on stands.

Victorian picture frames are copies of older frames. There was a great variety of nineteenth century frames and they relate to the various styles of furniture and decoration of the Victorian period. Victorian Empire frames were similar to those of the earlier Empire period. They were rectangular in shape with moldings of beading, acanthus leaf, Egyptian papyrus, and lotus leaf carvings. Some pictures in museums are still in their original frames and this is the best place to study picture frames, although reproductions of all period frames are to be had at the picture frame shop today. Since the French Louis XV was the most popular Victorian style there are many large Victorian picture frames of rococo design. These frames were wide and deep. They were

LEFT. Cast iron table mirror with crinoline figures. Patriotic trophy obelisk and flag on base. 1865–1870. (*The Index of American Design*) CENTER. Cast iron mirror frame, rococo design. 1850–1875. (*The Henry Ford Museum*) RIGHT. Cast iron dressing table mirror on stand. Renaissance design influence. 1850–1860. (*The Index of American Design*)

Gilt and gesso frame, leaf scroll border.

Elaborately carved frame. Renaissance design.

Carved and gilt frame, Elizabethan influence in corner motifs.

Rococo carved and gilt frame, acanthus leaf design. (*All frames, Robert D. Bunn*)

made of plaster carved with large flowers, leaves, and foliage borders which were covered with gold leaf. The frames were both oval and rectangular, but often an inner oval held the picture within the wide and heavy rectangular frame. All of the frames in a room were usually of the same design and these often matched the mirror frames and cornices so that there was an effect of dazzling gilt and exaggerated rococo design. Various designs of fluting, guilloche patterns, and criss-cross surface patterns often covered the flat surfaces of the gilt borders and smaller carved borders of grapes, oak, and laurel leaves alternated with the flat surfaces. Some frames were completely covered with a pattern of raised carving and others only had sprays of flowers or heavy cartouches at the corners of the frame.

American nineteenth century primitive paintings were framed in plain wood moldings painted flat black. They had a narrow gold leaf band on the outer edge and on the inner edge next to the picture. Sometimes the frames are marbleized and some frames have silver gilding instead of gold. In the late nineteenth century the frames were made of angular moldings and flat wood veneer or of black walnut with a small border of gilt or with burl veneer decoration. Small oval gilt and black walnut frames were made in the 1860's. They usually contained family photographs and were made of several sizes from 12 to 16 inches in diameter. There were also similar frames made of pine and gesso carved with fruit and flowers, sometimes as a crest at the top of the frame or in four clusters at the top, bottom, and sides or in a twining vine border around the frame. These frames were covered with gold leaf, not paint. Today they are inexpensive, especially the walnut ones containing old photographs which can be removed and mirror glass substituted. There are also many larger rectangular picture frames with heavy gesso leaf or scroll borders covered with gold leaf that will make attractive mirror frames. Late Victorian frames included the rustic tick-tack-toe of oak which have the corners crossed and fastened with a white china button instead of mitered. Carved rustic frames with machine-carved leaves set on their corners were made "for framing mottos." There were also frames of imitation marble, walnut, and ebony with raised white lines "engraved and gilt." Antique bronze,

LEFT. Walnut frame decorated with sliced walnuts. 1885. Made by Henry Ford. RIGHT. Oval pine frame with molded gesso fruit designs. 1850–1870. (*Both, The Henry Ford Museum*) BELOW. Carved rosewood frame made by Ernest Weber. c. 1857. (*The Metropolitan Museum of Art*)

natural wood, and imitation wood and plush-covered frames were also advertised in the 1880's. Walnut frames often had an inside narrow gold leaf molding. This was sometimes stencilled with geometric or vine borders. An unusual fretwork frame with criss-cross corners is made with borders of small hand-carved triangles of soft wood which form a design similar to Flemish 17th century frames. In 1854 *A Complete Guide to Ornamental Leather Work* was published in Boston. It included directions and designs for making mirror frames and other articles out of cut and modeled leatherwork. The frames were usually oval and the designs of leaves, fruit, and flowers heavily massed.

Lamps, Girandoles and Lusters

THE lamp evolved through scientific improvements on its combustive system and the subsequent changes of fuels from grease fat and whale oil to kerosene. The invention of the oil-burning Argand lamp in 1780 marked the real beginning of modern lighting, but the design and development of the lamp as we know it today was made in the nineteenth century. To collectors interested in the development of lighting the various scientific improvements and changes in the mechanical operation and the different fuels used are important, but from the standpoint of the collector of nineteenth century decorative arts the design of the lamp base and shade are the valuable considerations. Early lamp designs were patterned after candleholders. Indeed, it is only since the middle of the nineteenth century that lamps replaced candles. One of the first lamp designs was the brass candelabrum of metal with its tin shade. These were made both with single light sockets and a side standard, and with double and triple lights held by a center bracket. Although they were made as early as 1800 they continued to be made all through the century and are reproduced today.

The Argand lamp had a standard of metal, usually bronze, cast with classic designs including vase forms and acanthus leaves. Argand lamp shades were of frosted glass with cut crystal prisms. These lamps were made with both one and two burners. Although of earlier invention, the Argand lamp was used in America until the middle of the century, together with the Astral or Sinumbra lamps which were a

RIGHT. Argand-type tin sconce with stenciled decoration, 1825–1850. FAR RIGHT. Bronze Argand lamp with cut frosted shade, 1840–1850. (*The Henry Ford Museum*)

Astral lamp with marble base, frosted cut shade with prisms, 1850. Overlay lamps with frosted shades and prisms. Marble base, Sandwich type, 1860, 1875. (*The Henry Ford Museum*)

variation on the Argand lamp. These too were made of metal—brass, bronze or silver—with glass shades. The bases of these lamps followed the various furniture revival designs. They were made with dome and round glass shades.

These lamps and the Carcel lamp, which was similar, were the lamps used in the homes of the well-to-do until the middle of the century. The New England Glass Company advertised Grecian lamps and plain and ground chimneys for Astral lamps, and hanging prisms as early as 1825. In 1850, Archer and Warner of Philadelphia, manufacturers of lamps, girandoles, etc., advertised "Argand, Annular, Parker's Sinumbra, Quarrel's Sinumbra, Quarrel's Albion, Isis, Parker's Hot Oil, Keer's Fountain and Carcel lamps." Such was the wide variety of fine lamps obtainable at the mid-century. Cornelius & Co. of Philadelphia had invented and patented the Solar lamp in 1843 and these lamps are marked with their trade-mark and the patent date. The lamps had round wicks, bulb-like chimneys and globe or flaring white or colored glass shades cut or sand-blasted in floral designs and hung with cut crystal prisms. The standard was brass and the base marble. But lamps were also made of many less expensive materials such as tin, iron, pewter, britannia; and later pottery, china, and glass of all kinds.

One of the most important branches of glass making in the nineteenth century was the manufacture of glass lamp bases. The Victorian lamps made in the greatest quantity were of glass and metal. A great number of lamps were made of blown and pressed glass. Blown lamp bases were plain or mold-blown, overlay, and cut. Some lamps have all types of glass techniques combined. The first glass lamps were blown in spherical or conical shapes. The reservoirs were ornamented with ribbing and panel molding and often cut and engraved. When pressed glass became popular some of the blown glass lamps had bases of lacy pressed glass which was made in a cup-plate mold. These lamps are extremely rare. From 1835 to 1860 pressed glass lamps were heavier

Clear pressed glass table or chamber kerosene lamps, 1875–1900 (*The Henry Ford Museum*)

and their design was influenced by the decorative trends of the period, which included Gothic and Renaissance motifs. Classic columns formed the stems, and the bases were made up of architectural moldings. The dolphin candlesticks and lamp bases in various colors belong to this period. Lamp bases were also made in amber, canary, greens, blues, amethyst, and clear and opaque white, and combinations of color were used on one lamp. These lamps were fitted with whale oil burners of pewter or brass. The glass fonts were conical, cylindrical, or hexagonal with heavy molded panels of simple motifs such as loops, circles, and ellipses. The bases were round, square, hexagonal and octagonal. The early Bigler, Arch, Circle and Ellipse patterns, and Pedal and Loop belong to this period. The Peacock Feather, Argus, Block and Thumbprint, Harp, Bull's Eye, and Fleur de Lys were also early patterns. These lamps were made at the New England Glass Company; Sandwich Glass Company; McKee Brothers; and Bakewell, Pears, and Company, but it is difficult to attribute any lamps to a particular company as designs were not the exclusive property of any one company.

Overlay or cased lamp bases combined one or more colors of glass overlaid on the clear glass, and they were decorated with a bold cut design of circles, ovals, stars, or diamonds. The contrast of the brilliant color of the overlay glass and the clear crystal of the cut design gave an exquisite effect. These lamps were made in the 1850's and 1860's and were never common. They were made mainly at the New England Glass Company and at the Sandwich Glass Company. The majority of those made at the New England Glass Company were ruby on a base of clear glass while those at Sandwich were made in a variety of colors including green, pink, rose, amber, blue and turquoise on clear glass. A Cranberry glass lamp was covered with a white overlay dotted pattern and has a milk glass column and base. A lamp of midnight blue entwined ribbon design has a column and base of pressed milk glass. The majority of these glass bowls were mounted with metal and were set on fluted metal or glass stems and fastened to marble bases. Over-

Kerosene lamp with pressed glass font and cast iron statuary base, 1875–1885 (*The Henry Ford Museum*)

lay lamps are popular and very expensive today, but they have also been reproduced and the collector must be cautious. There were also lamps with translucent colored bowls decorated with a vine design in gold, and lamps with bowls of a Venetian looped pattern of clear and opaque color. These bowls are round, oval or square and are mounted with metal and usually set on a square or round base.

Later lamps, although pleasing in color, were sold in parts and assembled by the lamp manufacturer so that they are not always well proportioned. Shades and prisms were also sold in lots and assembled with lamp bases in the warerooms. Kerosene lamps had large globular fonts blown in molds, the bases were pressed and the parts were connected with brass collars. The square or curved feet were black or white opaque glass. These opaque or translucent colored lamps were made in many varieties and sometimes gilding was added.

The late pressed glass lamps were made to burn kerosene and their fonts were round and larger, and the lamps were taller. Some had cast metal stems with cherubs or other figures. The late pressed glass lamp patterns included Ribbed Ivy, Stedman, Bellflower, Fine Rib, Ribbed Palm, Prism, Sawtooth, Hamilton, Cable, Honeycomb, Sandwich Star, Prism and Flute, and others, although lamps were not made in all pressed glass patterns. In 1876 both standard lamps and squat lamps with handles were made in the Emblem pattern, which had impressed United States flag shields around the lamp font. The metal collars have the inscription: "Pat'd Apr. 19, 1875. M'ch 21, 1876." Many lamp chimneys also have the Emblem design.

The Actress, Three Face, Frosted Leaf, and Lion pattern lamps belong to the 1880's. Pressed glass lamps of various sizes in the coin pattern were made at Wheeling, West Virginia, in about 1892. These were made in both clear and opaque milk glass. There were many other milk glass lamps of all sizes, some with glass bases and others with cast brass or bronze bases. The tall, slender rose bowl lamp is the most attractive. A squat lamp has a panelled poppy design and another

Pattern glass lamp with dark green font and green shading, at top of glass shade. After 1860. (Ruth Little: *Old Lamps and New, Restoring and Decorating*)

small lamp has a pansy panel. Milk glass lamps were made in combinations of clear and colored glass, but seldom in two different colors of milk glass. There were many miniature milk glass lamps, the most common being the little Cosmos design lamp. There were miniature Pansy design and Block and Circle design, which were also common. These lamps were made with pressed milk glass chimneys of the same design and with plain clear glass chimneys.

Miniature lamps were also made in many clear pressed glass patterns. They were designed to be used as night lights in bedrooms but were also used as "sparking" lamps. When the small amount of oil was burned out it was the hour for the suitor to depart. These lamps, which measured from 4½ to 8 inches tall, were made in great quantities at the end of the century. Miniature lamps were also made in various types of fancy glass, such as satin glass. Other types of small lamps include the Acorn lamp made by Hobbs, Brockunier, and the Fairy Lamp. Fairy Lamps were mostly of English make, although the Phoenix Glass Company of Pittsburgh, in the 1880's advertised Art Glassware, Pearl Satin Glass, and "sole manufacturers of Fairy Lamps in U.S." According to Amelia MacSwiggan, author of *Fairy Lamps*, Samuel Clarke manufactured fairy lamps in Newark, N.J., 1884–88 and Houchin Co. in New York City in the 1880's.

There are several types of lamps that came into use after the middle of the nineteenth century, and these old kerosene lamps are the most characteristic Victorian lamps. The earlier peg bowl lamp had been made to fit into a candlestick, but now they were made to fit into glass, metal or marble bases. Small glass hand lamps with a loop finger-hold were made in great numbers. These lamps had a glass chimney but usually did not have a shade. Similar lamps also were made to fit into metal wall brackets. These were designed with fonts of clear glass or in opalescent, cranberry or hobnail glass, and often had ball or fringed petticoat shades to match. The Rayo lamp, a variation of the hand lamp, was made of brass and at first was only equipped with a chimney, but later had a tripod metal holder for a student or Tam O'Shanter shade. The student lamp was another type that was popular late in the century. These were made of metal, with a central stem set on a base and with branches to hold the font and shade on one side and the oil tank on the other. Sometimes the oil tank and font are of glass and recently in a Vermont shop I saw such a lamp with shade and oblong cylinder oil tank painted with the well-known scene of heron and cattails.

ABOVE LEFT. Brass Student Lamp with double burners and green glass shades, 1890–1915. LEFT. Bronze double Student Lamp with green and white overlay glass shades, c. 1900. ABOVE. Brass Student Lamp with green shade, 1890–1900. (*The Henry Ford Museum*)

Hanging lamp with opaque white shade, c. 1875. Hanging lamp with painted glass shade and prisms, 1890–1900. Hanging lamp with hobnail ruby glass shade, c. 1890. (*The Henry Ford Museum*)

The hanging library lamp with glass or metal font, a glass chimney and a glass shade with prisms was set in an adjustable metal frame. A small metal dome hung over the chimney to protect the ceiling. The shades of these lamps were often elaborate and decorative. Some are hand-painted, others are made of hobnail, Rubena Verde, or other colored glass with the border of the frame set with colored stones and prisms. Stem lamps with fonts of pressed or hand-painted glass or china set on a cast brass base were made in the 1880's. These had glass chimneys and ball or Tam O'Shanter shades. The stems were sometimes elongated and cast in the shape of a head, naked child or fluted column. Other stems were cylinders of china decorated with hand-painted flowers. Late in the century a tall brass floor lamp with molded brass bowl and hand-painted ball shade was made. These lamps were sometimes made with tripod legs but more often the lamp rod was set in the center of a small square three-tiered brass table.

Shades on Victorian lamps were of various types and shapes as well as different kinds of glass. There were round ball shades, Tam O'Shanter shades with wide flare and small neck, student shades with rounded flare; and pleated petticoat shades and crimped shades. The shades were plain or tufted and were made of various types of glass including satin, cranberry, opalene, coralene and overlay. Patterns included thumb-print, hobnail and candy stripe. Lamps made in the various types of Victorian Art Glass included a Burmese table lamp made by Mt. Washington Glass Works in 1886. There were also frosted and clear designs and shades with embossed patterns of flowers and all-over designs.

There were many glass companies making shades for lamps, including Gillinder & Sons, who made "etched, cut, sandblast and opal shades and globes." The Novelty Art Metal Company of Brooklyn advertised "Art Bent Glass Globes" in 1897. The Washington Flint Glass Company of Philadelphia made shades decorated with cupids, butterflies, and flowers; and the Murray Flint Glass Works also made colored globes and shades, "Opal Tinted and Windmill Rococo." They also made lamp fonts. Silver etched banquet globes and etched top chimneys were made by F. Horman & Co. The Rochester Lamp Company made lamps decorated with painted scenes, including windmill decorations. Decorated lamps were also made by the Eagle Glass Company, who advertised a Gone-with-the-Wind type of lamp with font and shade decorated with roses. A Venus decorated lamp was made by Thos. Evans of Pittsburgh.

However, the most popular lamp in the 1880's and 1890's was the parlor or so-called Gone-with-the-Wind lamp which had a large globular glass base and a matching globe-shaped shade. The base and shade were usually painted or heavily ornamented with Lalique-like patterns of raised flowers. Glass prisms often hung from the shades. These lamps were also set on rococo stands of openwork cast bronze or

LEFT TO RIGHT. Stem lamp with pattern glass font, pressed Tam O'Shanter shade with prisms. The stem is opaque glass with painted decoration, the base black iron, c. 1880. (*Ruth Little*) "Gone with the Wind" lamp with frosted ruby pressed glass font and shade, 1875–1885. (*The Henry Ford Museum*) Lamp with brass rococo design font and base. Shade frosted pressed glass, 1875–1885. (*Carren Ltd.*) Parlor lamp with painted wild rose decoration on shade and base, 1875–1890. (*The Henry Ford Museum*)

brass. There were also smaller lamps with Dresden china bases, and china lamps for home decorating could be purchased from the Summerville Glass Works and from the Phoenix Glass Company. They also had cream-colored porcelain table and banquet lamp fonts of Limoges and Vienna porcelain available for decorating. E. Aulich of New York, who operated a shop for painting lampshades, was also a teacher of china painting and his design for a globular china shade was illustrated in the *China Decorator*, April, 1900. Some china lamps also had flaring shades. These shades, too, were hand-painted. A familiar small lamp with a tubular base and dome shade had a hand-painted landscape including deer. It was made by the New England Glass Company and the shade was painted by George L. Noyes who was employed to do hand-decorating and who afterwards became a Boston artist of note.

LOWER LEFT. Lamp with cast bronze base with angel heads, Gothic design on font and frosted glass globe. Boston and Sandwich Glass Co., Sandwich, Mass., 1875. (*The Henry Ford Museum*)

Other popular painted lamp base designs included the heron and cattails, Cabin in the Snow, the shepherd scene, Paul and Virginia, bunch of grapes, and wild roses. A rare Burmese lamp has a scene with flying ducks hand-painted on its font and Tam O'Shanter shade. Parlor Lamps with metal bases were also popular and there were also tall banquet lamps with pierced brass and bronze rococo designs, and Renaissance designs with heads in ovals. These tall decorative lamps had a hand-painted or Lalique-like ball shade. Late in the nineteenth century lamp bases and shades were made of cut glass. There is a rare cut glass lamp in the Cobweb pattern, but lamps of Russian, Hob Star, and other deep cut patterns are more common.

Elaborate gold and silver lamp bases were illustrated in the Reed and Barton catalogue of 1885. The designs were a combination of Oriental flower and bird motifs and sculptured Renaissance figures

LEFT TO RIGHT. Brass parlor lamp with hand-painted student shade, c. 1900. (*Ruth Little*) Rochester burner, kerosene lamp with Japanese design bronze base and floral decorated globe, c. 1900 (*The Henry Ford Museum*) Lamp with silver or gold plate in Venetian design. Passion flower design on font and bird and floral decoration on globe. (*Reed & Barton Catalogue, 1885*) ABOVE. Lamp base and globe, cut glass Sunburst pattern, 1900. BELOW. Lamp base and globe, prism pattern 1892. Owens-Illinois Glass Co. (*The Toledo Museum of Art*)

and acanthus leaf scrolls. Globes and shades were purchased separately and the decoration of the shades included birds, butterflies, flowers and landscapes.

Tiffany lamps were first sold in 1895. Some bases were of Favrile glass with mother-of-pearl shades. Others were a combination of bronze and Favrile glass. Among the first designs were the tall-stemmed bronze candelabra in Queen Anne's lace pattern and the dandelion lamps. The earliest of these were made for kerosene and marked with the monogram of the Tiffany Glass and Decorating Company. The same designs were later marked "Tiffany Studios, New York." The Tiffany dandelion lamp and the dragonfly lamp were exhibited in Paris in 1900. The bronze base with leaded glass shade was so popular that it was copied both in America and abroad. The bases as well as the shades varied in design. Among the best known leaded shade designs were the group of flower designs including wisteria, grapes, daffodils, water lilies, peonies, poppies, wood anemones, ivy, pansy,

Tiffany lamps: LEFT. Daffodil, gilded leading and base. CENTER. Dragonfly, shades of amber with vari-color eyes. RIGHT. Twelve Branch Lily. (*The Chrysler Art Museum of Provincetown*)

rose (either red or yellow), leaf, orange petal, geranium, butterfly, tulip, tree, and geometric. Other types included the Scarab, Snail, Turtleback, Mushroom, and Spider and Web. The lamps were marked "Tiffany Studios, New York" on either the top or bottom rim of the shade. There were also candelabra lamps, including the lily-cluster design with morning-glory shades.

The shapes and decoration of the Tiffany pottery also suggested plant and flower forms. The earliest of the pottery bases was deep ivory shaded with brown. Later shades of green were used and some had a mat glaze which gave a crystalline effect. Each piece of pottery was marked "L.C.T." on the base. There were also Tiffany glass shades for hanging lamps and the designs Chestnut, Tyler, and October Night were often copied. Tiffany lamps were never cheap. They ranged in price from $100 to $750 when made. Today, again, they are expensive and in great demand. Copies or similar glass shades are quite common, but not cheap. Lamp shades were also made of Quezal and Carnival glass. Tiffany also fitted shades to pottery lamps made by the Grueby Faience Company of Boston, but after the failure of the Grueby firm, Tiffany Studios began to make pottery bases.

Pottery lamp bases were also made of Rookwood Pottery and since Rookwood was sold at the Tiffany Store undoubtedly some Rookwood pieces were fitted with Tiffany glass shades. The Chesapeake Pottery of Baltimore, Maryland, made parlor and banquet pottery lamps with adaptations of classical designs, and the Pauline Pottery of Edgerton, Wisconsin, made candlesticks and lampstands with hand-painted designs in the Japanese manner. According to Barber, Goodwin Brothers of Connecticut made "fancy lampstands, hand decorated in colored and rustic designs bronzed, silvered, and lustred."

Candelabra lamps with wick burners for camphene or whale oil were set on four to six metal branches ornately decorated with acanthus leaves, grapes, and cupids. There were also many candelabra of bronze and other metals in rococo styles which were made for mantel sets. Sometimes these came in combinations with two candelabra and a matching clock and while many were made abroad there were also such sets made in America. These were advertised in 1853.

Set of lusters for mantel garniture. Brass stem with Mother and Child in grape arbor set on marble base. Prisms hang from candleholders, 1840–1860. (*The Henry Ford Museum*)

The metal candelabra or girandoles with cut glass prisms which were known as Paul and Virginias were the popular ornament for the Victorian mantel shelf. These gaudy fixtures set on a marble base were made in single and branched forms and also in sets of three pieces. The cast gilt-metal figures included not only Paul and Virginia, but Robinson Crusoe, Columbus, Lancelot, Paul Revere, Robin Hood, Pocahontas, the Crusaders, George and Martha Washington, Joan of Arc, a hound, a vase, a basket of flowers, lovers, Jenny Lind, and a Gothic cathedral. The prisms for these and other lamps and candelabra were mostly made in Brooklyn, New York, and Meriden, Connecticut, but they were also made by T. G. Hawkes Glass Co.; Libby Glass Co.; C. Dorflinger & Sons; L. Straus & Co.; and the Mt. Washington Glass Works. There were also bronze candelabra with Parian figures.

Lusters were also popular mantelpiece garniture. Lusters were made of various kinds of glass, including clear, frosted, and opaque class, enamelled and cut, and were hung with prisms. By inserting a candle the luster became a candlestick. While many lusters were made in France and England they were also made at American glass factories and the prisms too were cut in American shops. Prisms were cut in many shapes. Victorian prisms are long triangular spears with spearhead, arrow, or dumbbell ends.

Collectors of decorative lamps are most interested in miniature lamps, Fairy Lamps, and pressed glass lamps. These lamps are comparatively small, colorful, and give an opportunity to assemble a collection of the various types of glassware and of the many different patterns of pressed glass. Prices of these lamps vary with popular demand. Lamps of any art glass such as Satin, Peachblow, Burmese, Amberina or Mercury glass are rare and expensive. Miniature lamps are usually more expensive than larger lamps because there were fewer of them made and they are in great demand. Collectors of larger lamps are more than likely collecting the lamps for use in the home rather than collecting pieces for a cabinet. The most expensive Victorian lamps that can be adapted for present-day use are the overlay lamps made by the New England Glass Company and the Sandwich Glass Company. These are very expensive. In fact, any lamp known to have been made at any particular company is more expensive than the same type lamp not authenticated. Although Argand, Astral, and Solar lamps are not cheap, there are still bargains to be found and these lamps often have the maker's name. So far they have not been in great demand with collectors. The lamps made late in the century which are truly Victorian in taste and spirit are just beginning to have collectors' attention. When more is known about the makers and decorators these will be more valuable.

Crown Milano lamp base and globe. Soft pink ground decorated with sea gulls, gold scrolls, stars and circles. Mt. Washington Glass Company. (*Flying Horse Antiques*)

Rogers Groups

IN 1859 John Rogers exhibited a small clay group of figures called "Checker Players" which was so well received that he decided to continue sculpture as a profession. Between 1859 and 1892 when his last group was put on the market, Rogers had executed over 80 groups and sold over 100,000 plaster reproductions. The plaster groups of John Rogers expressed the spirit of the American Victorian era. They satisfied the people's love for sentimental story-telling art. Although Rogers was a man of culture he was close to the people in his homey interests, and his artistic ideals were those popular with the majority of the people. Thus thousands of his groups sold and a Rogers Group sat on a table, shelf, or pedestal in every middle-class parlor in America at the end of the century. Rogers is remembered today not because he was a great sculptor but because he pictured in detail the America of his day. His realistic groups depict the costumes, the furniture and the social activities of a century ago. For this reason Rogers Groups are interesting and worth collecting today. The subject matter of Rogers Groups had popular appeal for they were close to the life of the people, the topics and day to day activities of the people.

Many groups were inspired by the Civil War, but even here he chose subjects that were near to the heart of the people rather than scenes of great battles. These groups included "Taking the Oath," "Parting Promise," "The Home Guard," "Camp Life," "Camp Fire," "The Wounded Scout," "The Returned Volunteer," "Sharp Shooters" and "Union Refugees." "The Fugitive's Story" which depicts a Negro slave holding a child telling her tale to the well-known abolitionists Whittier, Henry Ward Beecher, and William Lloyd Garrison; and "Council of War' which includes portraits of Lincoln, General Grant, and Secretary of War Stanton have more monumental subject matter. In fact, this latter group was suggested to Rogers by Stanton in his letters to John Clifford who wrote to Stanton at Roger's request. The scene as suggested by Stanton was the conference after Grant's return from the visit to the Army of the Potomac. After receiving a finished group Stanton wrote to Rogers April 1868: "I think you were especially fortunate in your execution of the figure of President Lincoln. In form and feature it surpasses any effort to embody the expression of that great man which I have seen." When "The Fugitive's Story" was completed in 1869 Garrison ordered copies, but also complained that his face was made "too thin." The poet William Cullen Bryant wrote: "You have succeeded in a higher degree than almost any artist of the age in making sculpture a narrative art."

A number of Rogers' Groups illustrate popular stories of the day such as Rip Van Winkle and Ichabod Crane. Joseph Jefferson, the well-known actor, was the model for the Rip Van Winkle groups and also for "Fighting Bob" of Sheridan's *The Rivals.* There were also scenes from Shakespeare's *King Lear, As You Like It,* and *The Merchant of Venice* and a group of Faust and Marguerite.

Although the Civil War groups have a historical value and the dramatic and literary figures are a commentary on the literary and theatrical interest of the time, it was the homely domestic scenes that were the most popular and more of these groups were sold than any other, and it is for these scenes that Rogers is famous. The people liked the exact detailed story-telling pictures which reflected their own ideas and life. Also, the aim of nineteenth century artists was to tell a story or relate a picturesque incident with realism and this Rogers did with great skill although his work was inspired by higher ideals. He hoped that his figure of "The Landing of Norsemen" would be used "for public parks to inspire patriotism." And writing to Ellen Rogers he says: "I never feel satisfied after I have finished a merely humorous design." There are groups of children such as "We Boys," "Going for the Cows," "School Days," "Playing Doctor," "Hide & Seek,

Fighting Bob, by John Rogers, 1889. (*The New-York Historical Society*)

Whoops!" and "The First Ride." There are also home scenes like "Weighing the Baby," "A Frolic at the Old Homestead" and "The Tap on the Window," and romantic groups like "The Parting Promise," "Neighboring Pews" and "Coming to the Parson."

Rogers also did figures for the lawn including "Hide and Seek" and "Bubbles," and he made several designs of vases for plants. He was also interested in the placing of his figures. For the lawn figures he sold wrought iron pedestals for $10, and for the other groups there were brackets, pedestals and three-tier tables which were obtainable in black walnut, mahogany or ebony. Rogers made several groups in Parian marble and in bronze. In 1900 seven bronze groups including "The Council of War" and a figure of Abraham Lincoln which is now in Manchester, New Hampshire, were exhibited at the Metropolitan Museum of Art. Rogers Groups were also exhibited in other museums, and the National Academy of Design gave Rogers immediate recognition, but in 1955 Rogers Groups formed the center theme of an exhibit at a New York gallery entitled "Bad Taste." Today collections of Rogers Groups are owned by the New-York Historical Society, the Albany Institute of History and Art, and the Essex Institute. The

Weighing the Baby, by John Rogers, 1877.
(*The New-York Historical Society*)

Metropolitan Museum of Art owns two bronzes, a group "Wounded to the Rear or One More Shot," and a figure of George Washington.

Rogers Groups are marked with the date of the patent and "John Rogers, New York" stamped in the plaster. The name of the group was also impressed in the front of the statue base. The plaster is a soft grey color varying from pearl or slate grey to fawn, snuff and cinnamon brown. The color consisted of three coatings of oil wash which protected the surface from chipping. Metal supports were placed inside the plaster to strengthen the group. The average group is from 20 to 24 inches high. Earlier groups made before 1863 were smaller and later groups were larger, some as tall as 47 inches. Rogers Groups were sold in large numbers. Over 100,000 of these groups were made, so they are fairly common today in spite of their perishable material. "Checkers Up at the Farm" and "Coming to the Parson" were especially popular groups and these are not difficult to find today. Other groups like "The Watch on the Santa Maria" and "Fighting Bob" and "The Fairies Whisper" are harder to find. Certain groups are more interesting from the artistic standpoint than others, although generally Rogers' Groups are well composed even though much of the subject matter is

The Tap on the Window, by John Rogers, 1874.
(*The New-York Historical Society*)

trite and the value is thus in the picture of the age rather than any art significance.

Rogers, however, made some excellent portraits such as those of President Lincoln, General Grant, and Secretary of War Stanton in the group "The Council of War;" the portraits of Whittier, Beecher, and William Lloyd Garrison in "The Fugitive's Story" and of the actor Joseph Jefferson in "Fighting Bob." Rogers also made a special study of horses and fine figures of horses are in the groups "Polo," "Fetching the Doctor," "The First Ride," "The Elder's Daughter," "Going for the Cows," "The Peddler at the Fair," and "We Boys." When first made Rogers Groups were advertised from $5 to $25 and in the 1930's when they were beginning to be collected they could be bought for $30 to $40. Now they sell for $100 up. Of course, they should be in good condition, but small chips can be mended although this detracts from the value.

There were several groups by other artists made at the same time as the Rogers Groups were made, and since they were similar they have often been erroneously attributed to Rogers. Several of these groups were made by the Boston dentist Henry Forrest Libby. One of his groups "Conquering Jealousy" is marked H. F. Libby, Boston, Copyrighted. Other groups were made by C. Hennecke & Co., Milwaukee, Wisconsin, a manufacturer of statuary and garden vases. This firm put out a catalogue for "Hennecke's Florentine Statuary" and listed "antique, Roman, Medieval and modern statuary, also 205 busts of celebrated personages." The statuary was made of various materials and included groups such as "Uncle Toby and the Widow," and "Faust and Marguerite" which are similar to Rogers' Groups. The Faust and Marguerite is stamped "C. Hennecke's Copyright" on the base. While these groups are not to be confused with Rogers Groups they themselves are interesting collectors' items. "Tannhauser and Lohengrin," "Minerva" and "Faust and Marguerite" were advertised in the Century Magazine 1886, 1887, and 1889, for $12, and a figure with Mother and Child called "Protection" sold for $8. There was also a figure called "Consolation" and a folksy figure called "Fairy Tales." The description of this figure is a commentary on the age and its attitude toward "Art." " 'Fairy Tales.' 20 inches high. A new group. Price $8.00. Rosy, buxom, and in spite of her years ever young in mind. Grandmother is at her favorite occupation, peeling potatoes. Her two grandchildren cling to her with stormy appeals to 'tell just one more of those beautiful Fairy Tales.' And grandmother smiles with that benign sweetness that is born of a kind heart and tells them for the fiftieth time the well known, old ever new story of Snow-White."

J. J. West of Chicago also made statuary groups. His groups were mainly of children. One group of a boy and girl was called "Getting Mad," another "Making Up." Other groups were "Playing Grandma," "Red Riding Hood," and "The Lost, Found" which was a figure of a girl with a lamb in her arms and a dog standing beside her. It was 20 inches high and sold for $6.00. Each group had its title stamped on the front of the base and "West's Statuary" was stamped on the bottom of the base. West sent out a catalogue and the statuary was sold in shops throughout the country. These groups would be interesting to collect along with the Rogers Groups.

Faust and Marguerite, Casper Hennecke Group, 1886.
(*The New-York Historical Society*)

Currier and Ives, and Other Lithographs

THE lithograph was the most popular type of picture hung on the walls of the average American Victorian home. There were also wood and steel engravings of well known paintings. But the lithograph, and especially those of Currier and Ives, gained the favor of most people, not only because they were cheap, but because their subject matter related to everyday life. Here are recorded the scenes, and contemporary events, and the doings of every day in the life of the average household of the second half of the nineteenth century. These prints have long been collected for their historical and commercial value and today they enjoy a popularity never before known. Nathaniel Currier, who had been apprenticed to several earlier lithographers, started

Spring, 1870, Currier & Ives. (*The Old Print Shop*)   The First Ride, Currier & Ives. (*The Old Print Shop*)

business for himself in New York in 1835. In 1857 he took James Merritt Ives into partnership. After this date until the firm closed in 1907, the prints were marked "Currier & Ives." Lithographs are drawn on stone with a greasy crayon, then transferred to paper by pressure of a press. The Currier & Ives lithographs were printed in black and white and hand-colored until about 1880, when they were generally printed in color from a series of stones. However, some early lithographs were printed or partially printed in color.

Currier & Ives prints offer such a variety of subject matter that there is a group of interest for every collector. There are rural scenes, farm and winter scenes, Mississippi River scenes, railroad, clipper ships and steamships. Sports such as hunting and fishing, baseball, yachting, bicycle racing, trotting and horse racing are other groups. There are scenes of fires and firemen, wrecks and disasters. The series of prints on the Revolution, Civil War, and Mexican War include portraits of Washington and Lincoln. Some of the lesser known prints are the sentimental portraits, pictures for children, kitten prints, name prints, music, and fruit and flower prints. There was also a group of temperance and religious prints, certificates and family registers, and humorous prints.

There are over fifty railroad prints which give an interesting and important record of the development of the American railroad. The earliest print was called "The Express Train." It is a scene on the New York and Erie Railroad and shows an early locomotive without a headlight and logs in the tender which were used for fuel. The pictures of family groups are particularly interesting because they depict Victorian dress and interior furnishings. One print shows the historic Bloomer costume.

Currier never claimed that his prints were works of art, and some of the sentimental and religious prints were crudely drawn. However, some of the best artists of the time worked for Currier and their paintings were reproduced on the prints. The artists included George Durrie, A. F. Tait, Eastman Johnson, George Inness, George Catlin, Thomas Nast, C. H. Moore, J. H. Wright, James Butterworth, Napoleon Sarony, C. Severin, Charles Parsons, W. A. Walker, W. H. Beard, Franklyn

The Great Naval Victory in Mobile Bay, August 5, 1864, Currier & Ives. (*The New-York Historical Society*)

Bassford, Louis Mauer, Thomas Worth, Frances Flora Bond Palmer, and many others, Works of these artists are sought by collectors today and many of their paintings are to be seen in American galleries and museums.

Fanny Palmer produced more subjects than any artist employed by Currier & Ives. She worked on all subjects but horses. Her clipper ship prints are among the finest of the marines and her railroad prints rank among the finest of that group. She also did trout fishing and hunting scenes. "The Happy Family," one of the finest game prints, was her design. But she is best known for the flower print "Landscape, Fruit and Flowers" which was a familiar type of scene dear to the heart of Victorians. George Henry Durrie also supplied some of the most attractive prints. With the exception of "Autumn in New England/ Cider Making" they are all winter scenes. The best known subject was

"Home to Thanksgiving." Durrie's paintings can now be seen at Shelburne Village, Shelburne, Vermont, and in other museums and private collections. Louis Mauer did many of the horse racing and trotting prints, hunting, fishing, and western frontier scenes. John Cameron was also known for his horse racing prints. Many oil paintings of outdoor life by A. F. Tait were also used as subjects for prints. His "Life of a Hunter/A Tight Fix" is one of the most sought after and expensive prints today. Charles Parsons is notable for his clipper ship prints and Thomas Worth specialized in comic prints of white and Negro humorous incidents.

Some years ago a group of experts was asked to choose the best fifty Currier & Ives prints. Although the votes varied on the fifty they were all agreed on the first three. They were "Husking" from a painting by Eastman Johnson, "Maple Sugaring" by Arthur F. Tait, and "Central Park/Skating Pond" by Charles Parsons.

Over 7,000 different subjects were published by Currier & Ives and a total of 10,000,000 copies were sold. Currier & Ives prints sold for 20 cents each and sixty dollars a thousand when new. "The Hunter/A Tight Fix" sold for $3,000 a few years ago. Many prints have been destroyed or mutilated by having their margins trimmed, but hundreds are still in attics or storerooms and the owners are unaware of their value. If you find a print in such places and can buy it cheap, it is a safe bet, but a beginner should always buy from a reputable dealer when paying a high price.

There are certain things that a collector should know. First of all, although all prints are marked, only copyrighted prints are dated, but the various addresses of the firm provide an indication of the date. In the small folio prints which were colored by inexperienced girls, the colors sometimes run over the borders; also there are no tints or gradation of color. The large folios were sent to artists for coloring and more care was taken and tempera or opaque colors were used on the highlights. Prints vary in quality as well as subject, and condition also affects the value of a print. Many prints have been reproduced. Clipper ship and Darktown prints were also printed on the old stones after Currier & Ives were no longer in business. These prints are not reproductions, but they are worth much less than originals. The printing, paper, and coloring is inferior to Currier's work.

The beginning collector would do well to concentrate on children, sentimental name subjects, or moral or religious prints. These subjects are not in so much demand and are therefore less expensive. "Jonny and Bessie" shows two children with a slate, "Pet of the Family" shows a child laden down with Christmas toys. Other subjects with children are "Mother's Joy" and "Early Sorrow." Large head subjects include "Little Manly," "Sailor Boy," "Little Daisy" and the popular "Young America" showing a child with firecrackers. The series of name prints includes individual figures of young girls or men. Temperance prints showing the evils of drink, "The Fruits of Intemperance" and "The Fruits of Temperance" illustrate the contrast between a ragged family and a prosperous family.

There were other American lithographers, some of whose prints are earlier than Currier & Ives, and some are finer. These include Pendleton of Boston; Kellogg of Hartford; Endicott, and Sarony, Major, and Knapp of New York; P. S. Duval of Philadelphia; James S. Baillie; Kimmel & Foster and many others.

Lithographs that had their color printed by a series of blocks instead of being painted by hand were called chrome-lithographs or "chromos." While there were many cheap chromos there were two firms that produced works of quality. In 1854 W. Sharp & Son of

Dorchester, Massachusetts, produced a series of four prints of the water lily known as Victoria Regia. These were large folio size 15 x 21 inches. They are brilliant in color but without the objectionable glossiness of most chromos.

The best known producer of chromolithographic prints was Louis Prang & Co., of Boston, Massachusetts. Prang was a contemporary of Currier & Ives, but he was essentially interested in the reproduction of fine art rather than cheap prints. He, like Currier, employed some of the best artists to make his cards and advertisements and purchased outright the majority of the paintings that he reproduced. Prang is best known for his Christmas cards and sentimental Valentine, Easter, New Year, and birthday cards. These were publicized by competitions for the designs, and exhibitions of the cards were held at the Boston Fine Arts Gallery and the Chicago Art Institute. The Christmas cards have also been exhibited and written about in recent times. While many of these cards were by Mrs. O. E. Whitney, probably a staff artist, artists were selected for the fourth competition and they included such well-known names as J. Alden Weir, Will H. Low, Percy and Thomas Moran and Thomas W. Dewing.

However, the range of Prang chromolithographs was wide and included many types of pictures and subjects. Prang's catalogue, Spring 1876, includes the following headings: Landscapes, Animal Pictures, Figure Pieces, Portraits, Flower Pieces, Dining Room Pictures, Gems

Valentine Card (*New York Historical Society*)

Christmas and New Year Cards, Louis Prang & Co., 1870–1900. (*Hallmark Historical Collection*)

of American Scenery, Bouquets, Children, Imperials and Album pictures, Rewards of Merit, Sunday School Texts, Mottoes and Marriage Certificates. This gives some idea of the scope of Prang's output. Of course, the small cards with sentimental floral greetings included the favorite Victorian flowers such as calla lily, the rose, moss rose, violets, passion flower, pansies and lilac. There were also bouquets with combinations of flowers and small flower or moss crosses covered with roses and lilies, daisies, ferns or autumn leaves. Flower pieces included a series of "Easter morning" by Mrs. James M. Hart and Mrs. O. E. Whitney. There was an interesting "Flowers of Hope" by M. J. Heade, and "Flowers of Memory" by E. Remington. Later there were large prints of flowers including carnations, roses, wisteria, gladioli and many other varieties. There were also fruits in baskets and large branches of fruits such as oranges and plums and a design "Indian Corn and Apples." A series of fifteen chromos of chrysanthemums by the botanical artists James S. Callowell and Alois Lunzer was called "Princess Golden Flower." There was also a series of orchid pictures. Later flower lithographs were also made on satin.

Landscapes in the catalogue included Spring, Summer and Autumn by A. T. Bricher, and a group of New York and New England scenes by J. M. Hart, and California scenes by John R. Key, including "Golden Gate, San Francisco," "Cliff House, San Francisco," "Mt. Diablo," Lake Tahoe, Sacramento Valley, Santa Cruz Mountains, Big Trees and Yosemite. Louis K. Harlow also painted a series of California and New England scenes. There was a series of water colors of western landscapes by Thomas Moran, including Salt Lake and the Yellowstone geysers. Benjamin Champney did a series of New England landscapes, and "Sunset in California." A copy of the now famous Bierstadt painting "Sunset" is available in Prang chromo.

Children included a portrait of "Little Prudy" by Elizabeth Murray. Later, in a list of 1897 "Little Prudy's Brother" is listed. There were also barefoot children, Little Bo Peep, and Young Commodore. There were groups of babies, including Prize Babies by Ida Waugh. Eastman Johnson's paintings, "Whittier's Barefoot Boy," and "Boyhood of Lincoln" were included in a catalogue of 1869, as was George L.

Brown's "Crown of New England," a landscape, the original of which was purchased by the Prince of Wales. Animal pictures included dogs by Alexander Pope, cows by Thaddeus Welch, cats and kittens including a Girl with Kittens by J. Enneking, and chickens, ducks, quail, and deer by A. F. Tait. A picture of a pointer and quail, one of a spaniel and woodcock and one of deer, are marked "A.F.T." Two chromos of inferior sentimental character, "Cluck, Cluck" and "Take Care" are signed "A. F. Tait, N.A. 1891."

However, the most interesting category of chromos listed in the 1876 catalogue were the Dining Room pictures. Included were trout, pickerel, and dead game by George N. Cass, and dessert pictures by R. D. Wilkie, I. Wilms and C. P. Ream. The original of C. P. Ream's Dessert No. IV is now titled "Raspberries and Ice Cream" and, wrongly attributed to Harnett, is owned by Mr. O. B. Jennings of New York City. In 1874 Prang issued a series of twelve chromos of the trades.

Advertisement for Roessle Brewing Company. Lithograph by Prang from painting by Claude Raquet Hirst. (*From book of Prang proofs. New York Public Library*)

These were used as aids in teaching. They show the various American trades such as the Carpenter, Blacksmith, Tinsmith, Baker, Shoemaker, and Tailor. These prints are excellent and are sought for by museums.

In 1889 and 1890 Prang issued calendars with scenes of Boston, New York, Washington, Baltimore and Philadelphia. There were also series of small books of verse and pictures called Prang's Fine Art Books. These included Flower Fancies, Notes from Mendelssohn, The Night Cometh, Haunts of Longfellow, Home of Shakespeare, Golden Milestones, Golden Sunsets, and Autograph Recipes. Another series of pictures were of sentimental subjects, of The Wedding and nuptial felicity.

One of the most ambitious publications by L. Prang & company was a four-volume book, *The Native Flowers & Ferns of the United States*, by Thomas Meehan in 1887-1880. This was illustrated by Alois Lunzer. These botanical prints are decorative and worth framing and hanging separately, but the text of the book is also excellent and if kept "as is" will increase in value. A book on reptiles and one on wild animals was also illustrated by Prang.

Perhaps the finest color work ever done by Prang was the illustration of *The Oriental Ceramic Art Collection of W. T. Walters* published by D. Appleton & Co., 1897. This consists of ten volumes of some of the most beautiful color printing ever done and should once and for all dispel all slighting remarks about Prang & Co.'s chromolithography. In 1897 Prang also made prints of Winslow Homer's "Eastern Shore" and "North Woods" and thus started this artist on his way to fame. The list of other well-known artists employed by Prang and whose pictures were owned

Illustration from 1876 catalogue of Louis Prang & Co. Desserts No. III & No. IV are by C. P. Ream. See page 76 for original painting.

by the company include William M. Chase, Abbott Thayer, Elihu Vedder, Thomas Moran, A. Bierstadt, J. J. Enneking, George E. Brown, J. W. Champney and Benjamin Champney. The pictures were sold at auction in the American Art Association sale in 1892. Prints by these artists are well worth collecting, but perhaps the best buys for present day collectors are the series of Civil War campaign sketches by Winslow Homer and the Civil War scenes of sea and land battles done in 1885 and 1886 by the artists J. O. Davidson and Thure de Thulstrup. These include "Sheridan's Final Charge at Winchester," "Battle of Chattanooga," "Sheridan's Ride," "Battle of Fredericksburg," "Battle of Gettysburg," "Battle of Kenesaw Mountain," "Battle of Allatoona Pass, "Battle of Antietam," "Battle of Spottsylvania," "Battle of Shiloh," "Siege of Atlanta," and "Siege of Vicksburg," all by Thulstrup; and "Monitor & Merrimac," "Battle of New Orleans," "Battle of Mobile Bay," "Kearsage & Alabama," "Battle of Port Hudson," and "Capture of Fort Fisher" by Davidson. Davidson who was primarily a marine

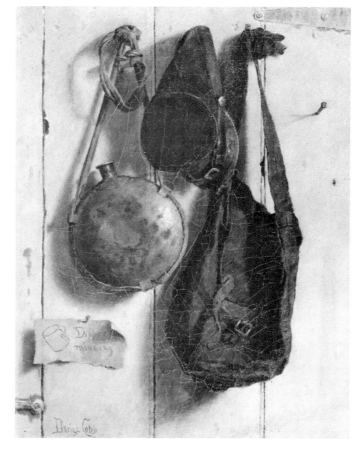

Civil War Still Life, by Darius Cobb,
Louis Prang & Co. Chromolithograph.

painter also did a series of Yacht Racing pictures for Prang which should be of interest to sports print collectors. The large print which Prang created in 1888 for the Old Army Friends Publishing Company from a painting by Darius Cobb is a trompe l'oeil with a battered soldier's cap, canteen, knapsack hanging against a door and at the lower left a piece of paper with an outline drawing of a tin cup and the inscription, "Dipper Missing." This is a collector's print, as is the still life of book, glasses, pipe, and candle, painted by Claude Raquet Hirst and lithographed by Prang for an advertisement of the Roessle Brewing Company.

In the 1890's Kurz and Allison of Chicago, Illinois, did an attractive series of Civil War prints. There are many of these available today and the prices are reasonable. In fact, at the present writing there is little demand for Civil War prints so if anyone is interested, now is the time to buy.

Colored fashion plates from *Godey's Lady's Book* and other women's magazines of the mid- and late-nineteenth century and flower, bird, and fruit prints whether hand-colored or chromolithographs are attractive when framed and hung in a group.

Fashion plate from Godey's Lady's Book, December, 1839. (*The New-York Historical Society*)

Primitive Painting

ALTHOUGH, contrary to the evaluation of twentieth century critics, there were many good artists in ninteenth century America, relatively few people could afford their paintings. Instead they had portraits, still life scenes, and memorial pictures painted by local artists. Some of them were crude and the best of them flat and somewhat distorted. Included among the primitives were scenes of local industry such as haying, corn husking, quilt making and landscapes, Grandma Moses' style. There were also religious themes such as the "Prodigal Son," "Moses in the Bullrushes," and memorial, allegorical, historical and patriotic pictures. Then there were family group pictures and single portraits. Some of these are large oil paintings and others are small water

Watercolor of family group in Victorian Parlor, c. 1875, Artist Unknown. (*The Henry Ford Museum*)

LEFT. "Lady with a Cat," oil on canvas. Mid-nineteenth century, Artist Unknown. (*Museum of Fine Arts, Springfield, Mass.*) RIGHT. Portrait of a Man with blue coat, water color, c. 1840, Artist Unknown, (*Colby College Art Museum*)

colors. For some years now these pieces have been collected because they have a certain simplicity, vigor, and decorative quality which appeals to present day art standards. At first they were cheap but as the demand has grown even the crudest primitive water color brings a price.

The most numerous of the paintings were the family portraits. Of these the family groups and children with toys are the most popular. These paintings, many done by craftsmen and itinerant artists, give us a picture of the nineteenth century. We see how the people dressed, and how their houses were furnished, what toys the children played with. They teach us American history not through facts and statistics, but at first hand through the faces and surroundings of the simple everyday people. These paintings are an authentic and important part of our national heritage. They are indigenous and perhaps the most truly American of all our art efforts.

Dickens on his visit to America recorded his description of American primitive portraits: "In the best room were two oil portraits of kit-cat size representing the landlord and his infant son, both looking as bold as lions and staring out of the canvas with an intensity that would be cheap at any price." The portraits can usually be identified by their vague stare. Hands if included are poorly painted, but the details of dress such as crimped bonnets, hair style, starched lace collars, and jewelry are painted in detail. Portraits often include books, flowers, chairs, tables, and other furniture as well as colorful carpets; children's portraits usually include toys such as dolls, wagons, pull or squeak toys and live cats or dogs. Still life paintings included a centerpiece with fruit, glasses, a knife, and perhaps a bottle or carafe of wine. All have an appealing period quaintness.

"The New Trick," Oil on canvas, by Charles Osgood. (*Vose Galleries of Boston*)

"Fancy Picture." Fishing, with waterfall, water color, c. 1845, Artist Unknown. (*Colby College Art Museum*)

However, in most cases the portraits are not likenesses but stereotyped blank faces and the painting is decoration, for many of these painters were sign painters and painters of clock fronts and mirror panels. The artist often varied his painting according to the price paid. The majority of the artists were unknown and those whose names are known are not always the best artists. William Prior was one who varied his likenesses with the prices, but today even his high forehead, large-eyed, flat portraits are expensive. Other primitive artists whose paintings are in private collections and museums today are Isaac Augustus Wetherby, Joseph W. Stock, Horace Bundy, Erastus Salisbury Field, Augustus Fuller and Joseph H. Davis and Eunice Pinney. Also each section of the country has its own primitive artists and more named and unnamed are being discovered each year.

Many of the religious and allegorical paintings were done in Female Seminaries. These were usually small water colors of such subjects as The Garden of Eden, Noah's Ark, The Prodigal Son, Moses in the Bull Rushes, or other stories from the Old Testament. The Lady of the Lake was a favorite theme as was the landscape with a Victorian house. There were also stylized landscapes and "Fancy Pictures" with figures fishing, or a shepherd or shepherdess.

The symbolical mourning picture which was often done in needle-work was also a theme for water color paintings. It included a tomb-stone with inscription "sacred to the memory of," a willow tree, and from one to a whole family of mourners. Many of these pictures date from early in the century, but the custom continued into the 1850's.

Any of the above mentioned pictures are expensive, but it is still possible to pick up small primitive water colors. There are water colors of ships and some collectors concentrate on these. Steamship

Victorian Landscape, Oil on canvas, c. 1875–1880, Artist Unknown. (*Colby College Art Museum*)

paintings by J. Bard who worked in New York in the 1860's are expensive, but there are many by unknown artists of the same date that are collectible. Often the name of the ship is given on the painting and the sails and rigging are sometimes reproduced with an authenticity to satisfy any sailor. However, often the painting is so stylized that the only realistic note is the name. Collections of ship paintings are to be seen in the Peabody Museum, Salem, Massachusetts; the Marine Historical Association, Mystic, Connecticut; Mariners Museum, Newport News, Virginia. There are also pen flourish pictures dating from 1850 to 1880's. These were usually done with a quill pen. They included pictures of horses, stags and other animals. There were books of directions and teachers who gave private instructions.

Sometimes primitive paintings were composed with stencils. Directions printed in a magazine of the 1840's gave information for the drawing and coloring which makes them related to our present day number paintings for amateurs.

Flower paintings and genre pictures painted by second rate artists and amateurs of the 1880's and 1890's are also being collected today. Flowers were not only painted on canvas but on silk tapestry, and on shiny black lacquered boards. Roses, violets, lilies, or a mixed bouquet in a Victorian vase were the favorites. Many of the paintings reproduced by Louis Prang and Company were painted by second rate artists who turned out typical sentimental Victorian arrangements of flowers. Some of these pictures were made from studio sketches, others were made from oil paintings, the most of which have disappeared from sight today, but there is still a chance that they will come on the market. For example, there are the "Strawberries and Baskets" and "Cherries and Basket" after Miss V. Cranbery, and the flowers by Ellen T. Fisher, Mrs. James M. Hart, Mrs. O. E. Whitney, Anne C. Nowell, Lisbeth B. Comins, Rosina Emmet, and Maud Stumm. Where is the original of Ida Waugh's "Prize Babies" and "Little Prudy" and "Little Prudy's Brother" by Elizabeth Murray; and where is "Before and After" showing a rooster fight by Leon Moran? These of course would be collected as typical products of the Victorian Age, not as examples of good painting.

Some of these painters although not well known are listed in Fielding and seem to have had a background of art training. Others were pupils of well-known artists or had an artist in the family who recommended them for reproduction work. However, most of their paintings which Prang reproduced were actually "gallery pieces" since many of them were included in the sales of Prang's collection of paintings at the American Art Association in 1892 and at Copley Hall, Boston, in 1899.

There were also pictures of historical significance painted by self-taught primitive artists such as John Lee of Newark who painted the Newark fire in 1845 and whose pictures, ignored by family and public for many years, are now in the Newark Art Museum and the New Jersey Historical Society. Such people as Lee found recreation in their painting as do businessmen, lawyers and doctors today. Their work is seldom better than second rate, but an occasional such painter strikes upon subject matter that has historical significance and paints in a style related to the primitives. Their paintings will be in the collections of tomorrow.

John Lee, Broad Street Fire, Newark, 1845. (*The Newark Museum*)

III. THE VICTORIAN DINING TABLE

DINING in America in Victorian times depended upon your status, your pocketbook and your locale, even as it does today. While there were several levels of dining, the main division was between those who set their tables with pressed glass and electroplate and those who could afford cut glass and silver. Pressed glass and plated ware were used on the tables of most middle class Americans along with gaudy cottage pottery, Willowware or Ironstone china with flowing blue or brown designs or gold decoration such as Wedding Ring, Tea Leaf, or plain Gold Band. Late in the century majolica became popular. Most of this china was made in England, but by the 1870's many factories in Ohio and New Jersey were making sets of ironstone, majolica and also more sophisticated china for the dining table. The sets usually included several sizes of plates, covered serving dishes, cups and saucers, crescent-shaped bone or salad dishes, butter pats, pitchers, and a teapot, sugar, and creamer.

Dining table at Sarah Jordan Boarding House, now in Greenfield Village. Turkey red table cloth, wild rose pattern, Greek key border. Tea leaf ironstone china. Silver plated caster with canary glass bottles. Daisy and Button pressed glass pickle jar in plated holder. Pressed glass goblets "Liberty Bell" pattern, Gillinder & Sons. (*The Henry Ford Museum*)

131

Along with this simple utilitarian china, pieces of pressed glass gave sparkle and variety. Pressed glass was mass-produced and cheap and it caught the popular fancy. Not all items of glass even late in the century were made in all patterns. Some of the patterns made after 1870 which include the largest number of items were Square Fuchsia, Beaded Swirl, Amazon, Art, Henrietta, Westmoreland, and Bar and Diamond. A typical list of items made in these sets included open and covered bowls, butter dishes, celery vases, footed compotes, cruets, creamers, decanters, goblets, pickle dishes, bread plates, salt and pepper shakers (individual salts were made in earlier patterns), sauce dishes, spoon holders, sugar bowls, syrup jugs, pitchers, wine glasses, and a wine set with jug and tray. Typically Victorian pieces were the spoon holder, celery vase, bread plate, pickle caster, and revolving center condiment caster. Knives and forks were of such silver or plated patterns as Fine Thread, or had bone or ebony handles.

In the center of the table stood the revolving caster stand of electroplate with its bottles of clear or canary-colored pressed glass patterns such as Daisy and Button, or thumbprint ovals with chased flower and leaf sprays. All dishes and silver were set on the table. Each place setting consisted of a plate, knife, fork and spoon, cup and saucer, and a napkin in a plated silver napkin ring. Above the plate was the bone dish and butter pat. A covered tureen held the meat or soup, and vegetable dishes were grouped in the center. The spoon holder, celery vase, pickle caster and covered butter dish of glass or electroplate with a cow finial, were placed at the corners of the table. Goblets or glasses were placed at each plate and a milk pitcher was usually on the table, while an ice water pitcher sat on a side table. The bread plate with its inscription "Give Us This Day Our Daily Bread," was a familiar item found on every middle class table. These plates were made in patterns of clear pressed glass and in opaque milk glass.

The simple family table with the above items was set on a turkey-red cotton damask cloth with gay patterns of flowers, fruits, birds and animals with a center medallion and fringed sides. These turkey-red cloths could be bought by the yard at such stores as Sears, Roebuck. Some cloths were also finished with fringe on all sides and ready for use. Most of these cloths were made in Scotland, Ireland, Germany and Austria, but some were also made in America. English designs included hunting scenes similar to but much less elaborate than the cloth illustrating a stag hunt which was used by Queen Victoria in Scotland. Other designs included oak leaves and acorns, cathedral, king's rose, pond lilies, poppies, shamrock, violet, and calla lilies.

Cotton damask table cloth, green and brown, J. Cunningham, New Hartford, Oneida Co., N.Y. 1841. (*The New-York Historical Society*)

A design of wild roses had a lavender border with a gold stripe. A cloth with a spread eagle in the borders was probably American, as were the field daisy, grape, cloverleaf, azalea, cherry, strawberry, nut and fern patterns. There was also a spinning wheel pattern, a wild horse in a tropical forest, and one with Egyptian motifs. A chrysanthemum pattern was also popular. These cloths had medallion centers and Roman Key borders. The colors ranged from turkey-red to soft pink and coral. They were used after the Civil War, and sold at Woolworth's in 1879 and at Sears, Roebuck in 1878.

Of course, the scale of dining graduated between the humble fare set on a turkey-red cloth and the satin damask, silver, and cut glass service supervised by a staff of servants. In between were those who had sets of Canton china or Wedgwood Creamware, heirloom silver and glass. In these homes fruit bowls of china or glass set on a pedestal usually replaced the caster in the center of the table. The compote might be made of clear pressed glass or of lacy-edged milk glass or it might be of imported English or French porcelain. Sometimes there was a mirror centerpiece set with porcelain figures, or for the country, a wooden platform with greens, rocks, and vases of flowers at the corners.

Jacob von Falke in the American edition of *Art in the House* (1879) gives directions for dining room furnishings. He suggests red for the walls, with one light over the table, and portraits, still life, fruit and flower paintings or animal and hunting subjects. The tablecloth should have a broad and rich border. Centerpieces include "flower and fruit

Silver plated fruit dishes. (*Reed & Barton Catalogue, 1885*)

dishes, vases, wine coolers, fountains, temples, statues, or girandolas."
Centerpieces in advertisements of Gorham and other silver manufacturers at this date included sculptured trees with birds and figures of
shepherds, rocky landscapes with deer and hunters, scenes of Paul and
Virginia, oriental temples and seascapes with Neptune and tritons.
A contemporary description of a dinner table in a Fifth Avenue mansion will give a picture of the affluence of the Victorian table of the
wealthy and notation of some of the actual items of silver, china, and
glass.

The following is partially paraphrased from an article in *Jewelers'*
Circular 1874: The centerpiece commanding and unifying the rich
array is a magnificent epergne overtopped with calla lilies bending
from lily chalices, and stems of gold which cluster over the central
basin, and three smaller basins hanging at equal intervals among the
drooping sprays and blossoms are also heaped and overhung with gay
flowers like the center. The surfaces of the four basins are of the soft
lustrous satin finish which the reader must have seen repeatedly to
imagine its beauty, deepened by the flash of narrow burnished bands
and moldings. The stem supporting these gorgeous hanging gardens is
a female figure, fashioned from one of the loveliest of classic models in
massive silver deadened to a pearly tint by oxidation, her feet poised
lightly on the cap of a temple dome that forms a pedestal for the whole.
On the dome is the consummate splendor of shaded and burnished zones
in contrast with sparkling engraved wreaths, glittering cornices, and a
frieze of rich oxidized bas-reliefs around the base, which rests on four
massive feet, as if it floated on the dazzling surface of a silver sea, or
more literally a burnished plateau as it is called, that mirrors back the
beauty. The plateau is oblong and sufficiently extended to float also
two graceful candelabra, one on either side of the epergne, with seven
branches bearing tall wax candles. Spaces for twenty-four guests are
marked off on the white damask by the sparkling cluster of glasses,
spoon, fork, and knife.

"The guests have a moment to admire the beauty of the new style
tureens, and the iridescent oxides and gold on the dainty little butterflies flitting over the edges of the silver salt cellars and the fanciful

forms of the chased pepper bottles and salad casters ranged within reach of every hand—for the old-fashioned omnibus caster is one of the particular vanities now fashionably dispensed with. All at once, at the secret signal of their chief the well-trained and well-dressed attendants appear, and in another moment the silver salvers come floating down before each guest." The bread is handed on plates which have a bas-relief of landscapes of golden grain with Ceres and her reapers, one of the symbolical works of art that hint the special purpose of each vessel. The salmon is served in a nautical dish with a trident fork and a sauce tureen with an enamelled shell spoon. The roast is served on the side-board. There too stand the wine-coolers, truncated columns of burnished silver twined with the cluster-laden vine and their bases sculptured with the mythology of Bacchus. All the vegetables of the season have their vessels in quadruplicate. The butter bowls with their covers and knives are appropriate silver and gold, crowned with symbols of bucolic fatness. Water pitchers, richly engraved, chased, and embossed with fountains, lakes and oases of palm, flanked by bowls of crushed ice, rimmed with pendant icicles of frosted silver and their bases pitted with rugged Arctic scenery in blocks and bergs and polar bears. The very ice spoon is perforated with an appropriate design. The salad bowl is another combination of lusters and sculptures. The classic olive in appropriate dishes; likewise the pickles with bladed silver forks. The celery vases are tall chalices.

At the pastry and dessert all the foregoing is removed and a fresh array still more elegant arrives. The ice-cream towers on massive silver stands sculptured with Arctic scenery to keep it from melting, with broad mirror trays beneath the knife-edged ice-cream spoon and the cool frost-finished saucers. There are also large vessels for fruit ices, with plates to match. The cakes and bonbons are on low comportiers. Grapes are served on a comportier with a design of fox and grapes and grape scissors are not forgotten. Fruits are on a silver barge. The elegance of the patterns of spoons, knives, and nut picks, and silver knick-knacks is only surpassed by the coffee service which the skillful engraver has used as a picture gallery.

The silver described above was all made by Gorham, but it was typical of the elaborate silver centerpieces and serving dishes also made by Tiffany, Black Starr and Frost, Caldwell, Samuel Kirk and other high class silver manufacturers of the time. Similar pieces were also made in plate by Reed and Barton, Meriden Silver-Plate Company, and Middletown Silver-Plate Company.

Snow white satin-like damask with a Dresden pattern of dancing cupids and garlands of flowers encircling the centerpiece set off the beauty of the silver and cut glass. This same tablecloth could be had in

Silver epergne with symbolic figures of Music, Art, Science, and Commerce. Exhibited at Philadelphia Centennial by Meriden Silver Plate Company. (*The Art Journal, 1876*)

color also. There were also tablecloths with designs taken from Royal Meissen china and tablecloths with colored borders of the Zwiebelmuster or Onion pattern were imported from Germany in the 1870's. There were also damask tablecloths hand-embroidered with monograms or crests in scarlet and blue with traceries of arabesque design. Different china was used with each course. Soup was served in Sèvres, entrées in English china, and fruit and coffee in Chinese or Japanese porcelain. Canton china long a favorite was still used on many tables. Minton china, French enamelled glass, Bohemian glass, Bombay striped glass and Stourbridge glass were also popular.

At the end of the century it became the custom to arrange flowers in the center of the table with small bouquets to detach and give to each guest. The nuts, preserves and bonbons were arranged around the centerpiece in small shell-shaped or basket dishes of silver, cut glass, or porcelain. Constance Cary Harrison in *Woman's Handiwork in Modern Homes* (1881) in her chapter on table decoration also notes that "American finger bowls and ice cream plates in clear blue, red, white, or Venetian thread pattern are $9.00 a dozen at Sandwich." The plateau or table mirror centered the table with china troughs filled with flowers and swans of Royal Worcester and Venetian glass on the mirror. A Dresden centerpiece of Cupid riding a swan was also used.

However, although no writer makes mention of them, there were elaborate centerpieces with branching vases or tiered bowls made at Sandwich in Tree of Life, Millefleur, and combinations of blue and white and yellow and white glass. Clarke and several other American manufacturers made centerpieces combining rose or tulip fairy lamps and tiny hanging vases. Flowers or greenery such as smilax were arranged at their base.

The ceremonious dinner of the 1890's was set on a tablecloth of lace over satin. Cut glass was in its heyday, and wine decanters of cut glass were set on the table and cut glass candlesticks with shades matching the tablecloth were set at each plate with cut glass vases holding violets for each guest. Sometimes there were tall banquet lamps of cut glass. The menus and place cards were of hand-painted silk. Bohemian glass goblets or goblets of harlequin glass, each a different color, were popular. Roman punch was served in the "hearts of a red rose or bosom of a swan or cup of lily or tiny life-saving boat." Tiny wheelbarrows, fans, or some other trinket served as favors. Majolica oyster plates were used, and hand-painted Minton china game plates, dessert plates with orchids and hummingbirds, and botanical fruit plates were popular. Ladies who did china painting painted plates with similar patterns.

The Society of Decorative Art had an influence on table decoration late in the century. Tea cloths and tablecloths with hand-drawn work, Japanese designs, crewel work, sprays of cyclamen, honeysuckle, and forget-me-nots, and cloths made up of squares of plush embroidered in crewel sprays were shown at their exhibitions. Cloths were also embroidered with borders of blue to match the china, and knife handles also matched. These were probably all Meissen Onion pattern. An amber silk table cloth had a design of Eastern embroidery, an old blue

LEFT. Marchian glass epergne with fruit and flowers. RIGHT. Silver Plateau with vase and cornucopias filled with flowers. (*Rustic Ornaments for Homes of Taste* by Shirley Hibberd, 1870)

Chinese bowl held yellow jonquils and roses, and dessert was served on oriental porcelain.

The Victorian dining table offers numerous items for collectors today. In addition to the better known articles of glass, china and silver, there are small objects such as napkin rings, knife rests, and butter pats, and in addition to patterns of nineteenth century silver there are knives and forks with bone handles and decorative and colorful porcelain handles. The blades of knives and serving forks and spoons are also cut and engraved in patterns which make them interesting collectors' items. Many articles can be picked out of junk heaps and forgotten attic trunks, but they can also be found in antique shops, for the dealers have been collecting from nineteenth century waste baskets for some years.

Dessert Molds and Pyramids

For special occasions the table decoration of flowers, crystal, and silver was augmented by centerpieces or pyramids constructed of pulled and spun sugar, nougat, gum paste and almond paste together with molds of various sizes and shapes set on socles or stands of nougat. The artistry for these elaborate concoctions was learned from the French. There were French confectioners in New York in the early nineteenth century. An advertisement of a confectioner gives us information about his products: "A. Lanniuer, Informs the public that he has completed a Monument in Sugar to the memory of the late illustrious, General Washington, which is for sale at his confectionary store in Broadway; in the front is a portrait of General Washington, and on each side the figure of Columbia weeping over his urn, with arms and appropriate trophies ..."—Mercantile Advertiser, February 24, 1800. Another advertisement describes the "Sugar Delicacies, which are made in a style alto-

LEFT AND RIGHT. Vases of pulled and spun sugar holding sugar flowers

gether new in this country. . . . He has likewise a new assortment of Table Ornaments, such as the Temple of Jedaus, and others, of an elegance superior to anything that has ever appeared in America; and in sufficient quantity to decorate a table of 500 covers. "Mercantile Advertiser," January 3, 1804. Ice cream was molded and sent out in various shapes by G. Chenelette & Co. according to their advertisement: Commercial Advertiser, May 9, 1801. These confectionary decorations were an accompaniment to formal dining in nineteenth century America and by the end of the century there were cook books giving directions for making elaborate and fanciful centerpieces. Full directions for the construction of centerpieces of many types is illustrated in *The Epicurean* by Charles Ranhofer of Delmonico's which was first published in 1894. In the chapter on Centerpieces or Pyramids, Ranhofer states that center-pieces were placed on the table to replace cold pieces in the third service of the French, and placed on the table at the beginning and at dessert for Russian style table service. The long list of subjects suitable for center-pieces includes Swiss cottages, temples, pavilions, towers, pagodas, mosques, fortresses, hermitages, belvederes, cabins, cascades, fountains, ruins, rotundas, tents, lyres, harps, helmets, boats, vases, cornucopias, baskets, beehives, trophies, and other military musical and agricultural subjects as well as trees, animals, flowers, and figures of famous persons. He then goes on to list suitable subjects from mythology such as "Cupid on a shell with swans;" "Neptune with tritons and Naiads;" "Venus teaching Cupid dancing;" "Apollo playing the flute, Jupiter watching." Biblical subjects such as Noah and the Ark are also suggested. Other suitable subjects included Normandy peasants dancing, a Tyrolian mountain climber, American Indian, and a Tartar on horseback.

Detailed directions for making some of the less pretentious pieces such as swans of various kinds of ice cream placed in a setting of pulled sugar, rushes and reeds and set on a socle or stand of nougat are included. The Helmet was a pudding made in a tin mold and decorated with ice

and set on stands of nougat. (*The Epicurean,* by Charles Ranhofer, 1894)

UPPER LEFT. Three-tiered molds filled with game mousse, set on a rustic stand made of nougats and topped by a stearine figure of Diana. UPPER RIGHT. "The Helmet", made of ice cream in a tin mold. The feather is of spun sugar. LOWER LEFT. Ice and ice cream molded in a swan mold and set on a base of reeds and rushes made of pistachio nougat. LOWER RIGHT. Dessert topped with stearine figure of Bacchus, intended for decorating the sideboard or as a centerpiece on the table. (*The Epicurean*, by Charles Ranhofer)

cream and pistachios while the helmet feather was made of spun sugar. There are directions for making a wheelbarrow filled with flowers which is constructed of various kinds of nougat, pulled sugar, fancy ices and glazed fruit. A windmill and a lighthouse are also both edible and decorative. Vases made of pulled and spun sugar holding sugar flowers and set on stands or socles of nougat and sugar were for table decoration only. Tiers of bonbons were also used as table decoration.

There were all manner of tin and copper molds available including melon molds, basket molds, horns of plenty, swans and a Bacchus on the barrel. The stands or socles were constructed by the chef, but there were stearine figures of birds, cupids, Diana, the Goddess of Liberty and other patriotic and mythological figures that could be purchased. Many fish, game and meat dishes were also constructed to be used as table decoration.

One of the interesting features of these centerpieces is their close resemblance to the decorative motifs of the era as seen on the silver, glass, and other accessories of the time. The themes also reflect the spirit and romantic ideas of the Gay Nineties. Although the molds and other cooking utensils used in making these fabulous contrivances were late nineteenth century factory items, they are nevertheless worth collecting. A few of them might still exist in the pantry of an old mansion and could possibly come up for auction. Also stearine figures although perishable may have been treasured and thus might be available to collectors.

Picturesque, story-telling food, a Victorian chef's masterpiece for serving pheasant. (*The Epicurean,* by Charles Ranhofer)

Blown glass birds, flowers and ships on cotton and tinsel rope under glass dome, c. 1875.
(*The Henry Ford Museum*)

IV. GLASS

Pressed Glass

PRESSED glass was made to imitate expensive cut glass. The diamonds, prisms, thumbprint, round lozenge and sawtooth cuttings of cut glass were all imitated and used in patterns of the cheaper pressed glass. Pressed glass was first made in the 1820's, and by 1840 factories for making pressed glass were springing up all over America. In the beginning, only necessary articles of tableware were made, but such was the popularity and demand for pressed glass that sets which included a great variety of pieces were made by 1850. The earliest pressed glass was made of lead flint glass, but after the Civil War pressed glass tableware was made of lime glass. Pressed glass was made in clear glass, but also in opaque white, black, and other opaque colors as well as marble glass, opalescent, and vaseline glass. The early pressed glass has a bell-like ring and is heavy and brilliant. The later lime glass does not have the ring. Also, early pressed glass is clear while much of the later glass is colored.

Almost all of the patterns of American Victorian pressed glass were made at the New England Glass Company in Cambridge, Massachusetts, and at the Boston & Sandwich Glass Company, but pressed glass was also made at several smaller New England glass houses, such as

145

the Portland Glass Company in Portland, Maine. In Philadelphia, James Gillinder & Sons made pressed glass, and in Pittsburgh there were several important manufacturers of pressed glass, including Bakewell, Pears & Co.; M'Kee Bros.; Bryce Bros.; Adams & Co.; George Duncan & Sons; and after 1891, United States Glass Company. The glass manufacturing center in Wheeling, West Virginia, included Hobbs, Brockunier, and Central Glass Company. There were also several companies in Tarentum, Pennsylvania; and in Ohio there were many glass companies, including Lancaster Glass Company, Bellaire Goblet Company; Nickel Plate Glass Company; A. J. Beatty & Co.; and Crystal Glass Company.

Most of the pressed glass made after 1850 belongs in the category of pattern glass which was made in matching sets for the dining table. A table set consisted of matching sugar bowl and creamer, butter dish and spoon holder. Later sets were made for a complete table service, with goblets and wine glasses, and many sets included such specialized dishes as salts, egg cups, celery vases, pickle dishes, jam jars and honey dishes, and the bread plate inscribed, "Give Us This Day Our Daily Bread." There were also cake plates on stands, caster bottles, footed compotes, cordial glasses, sauce dishes, champagnes and decanters in some of the popular patterns such as Bellflower.

In a book such as this, which covers many subjects, we can give only an outline of the glass patterns available and some of the characteristics of their design. Since the serious collector of pressed glass will want to own Ruth Webb Lee's book, *Early American Pressed Glass,* it seems best to follow her classifications. Mrs. Lee divides the various patterns into groups according to the similarity of their designs.

The first pressed glass patterns were the heavy simple designs which have more emphasis on form than surface pattern. These were made during the 1840's, but many of them continued to be made as late as the 1880's. Mrs. Lee calls this group Colonial. The glass is thick and the outlines bulky. There is a similarity between many of the patterns, which are made up of heavy panels, loops, ovals, and thumbprint motifs. However, there are differences even among the same patterns since they were made at several factories, and thus not only the design but the quality of the glass varies in brilliancy and weight. The Colonial group includes 17 patterns of which the following are the most popular: Ashburton, Argus, Excelsior, Petal and Loop, Diamond Thumbprint, Huber, and Washington. There are several patterns in this group such as the Sandwich Star, Four Petal, Sunburst, Waffle, and Thumbprint which are more decorative, and these patterns seem closer related to cut glass. Pressed glass was not marked, but must be identified by the quality of the glass and by acquiring familiarity with the various firms that made it and the patterns that they made. For example, the early Ashburton pattern was made at the New England

Diamond Thumbprint pattern pressed glass. TOP ROW, LEFT TO RIGHT. Rare pint decanter; rare expanded bowl on low foot with scallop & point rim; spooner with scalloped top & broad foot; compote with scalloped edge on low standard; water tumbler; rare whiskey tumbler; footed master salt. BOTTOM ROW, LEFT TO RIGHT. Decanter with stopper; compote with scalloped edge on high standard; celery vase. W. M. Guthrie Collection, Conestoga Auction Co. (*The Spinning Wheel,* April, 1966)

LEFT. Pressed glass celery glass, Bellflower pattern. RIGHT. Pressed glass goblet, Pineapple pattern. (*The Corning Museum of Glass*)

Glass Company in 1849 and at Bakewell, Pears & Co. Fragments of Ashburton have also been excavated from the site of the Boston & Sandwich Glass Company. Ashburton was made in twenty-two different articles, including bitters bottles, champagnes, clarets, cordial glasses and decanters.

The ribbed patterns also form an early pressed glass group. The simplest pattern, the Fine Rib, consists of fine vertical ribs which cover the surface of the glass, leaving plain stems on the glasses, compotes, and other footed pieces. Ribbed patterns with vine designs on the ribbed background are more decorative. These include the popular Bellflower, Ivy, Acorn, Grape, and the heavier, baroque Ribbed Palm and Inverted Fern. Bellflower was made in more pieces than any of the other patterns. It includes a rare cake plate, compotes, caster sets, butter dishes, pitchers, decanters, creamers, sugar bowls, salts, spoon

ABOVE. Pressed glass footed bowl, Horn of Plenty pattern. BELOW. Pressed glass bowl, Ivy pattern. (*The Corning Museum of Glass*)

Pressed glass, footed bowl, Lincoln Drape pattern. (*The Corning Museum of Glass*)

Blue Lincoln Drape syrup jug with applied handle and tin lid. Black glass plate, Gothic openwork edge. Rare electric blue covered sugar bowl, Four Petal pattern. (*The Henry Ford Museum*)

holders, plates, goblets and tumblers. There was also a variety of Fine Ribbed pieces and these plain ribbed articles could be combined to good effect with any of the other rib patterns. As with all pressed glass patterns the plates, wines and tumblers are the hardest pieces to find.

Other early patterns include the many variations of the Sawtooth. The earliest were heavy and coarse with points. Later there was a pattern with smaller points known as the Diamond Point, and still later the points were flattened, and this pattern was known as the Flattened Sawtooth. These patterns were made by many factories over a period of forty years. The early Sawtooth covered sugar bowl and compotes are especially graceful pieces. A toy set was made by Gillinder & Sons of Philadelphia for the Centennial.

The Bull's Eye and certain related patterns such as the Horn of Plenty, Comet, and New England Pineapple, were made in the 1850's–1860's. They are characterized by the large bull's eye circles which form the basis of the designs. These patterns are heavy in weight and bold in design and the glass is brilliant. The most popular of this group is the Horn of Plenty. A great variety of pieces were made in this pattern by the Boston & Sandwich Company and by M'Kee Bros. and others in Pittsburgh. There were several variations of Bull's Eye; Bull's Eye with Diamond Point, or Bull's Eye with Fleur de Lys. These more elaborate designs would be effective used together with the plainer Bull's Eye.

There are several patterns which were first made in the 1860's that are not only attractive patterns, but they are also interesting for their connection with historical events or happenings in the American scene. Gothic architecture and decorations were in style in America at about this date and the Gothic Pattern suggests the pointed arches of a Gothic church, while the pointed ribbings of the Hamilton pattern also suggest the Gothic motif. After the death of President Lincoln in 1865, the tableware pattern known as Lincoln Drape was made at the Boston & Sandwich Glass Company. It was made with a plain drape and also with a tassel, the tassel form being the rarer pattern. Another pattern, the Cable, was made in the 1860's to commemorate the laying of the Atlantic Cable. It is a plain simple pattern with a panel and borders of diagonal ribbing representing a cable. The Cable is a better design than the variant Cable with Ring although the plates in both patterns are attractive. These patterns are all of heavy brilliant glass and have a clear ring. There were also many varieties of Thumbprint and Honeycomb made in the 1860's. These are simple heavy patterns that relate to the Colonial group.

Between 1870 and 1880 a group of grape patterns was made. While the grape and grape leaf have always been a favorite motif with glass makers, it is interesting to note that these grape patterns were made at a time when naturalistic design was especially popular in

Westward Ho footed bowl and covered butter dish, Gillinder & Sons, c. 1870's. Goblet, Frosted Deer and Dog pattern. (*The Henry Ford Museum*)

America. There were grape designs in wrought iron and on the carved wood chairs, sofas, tables and beds of Belter and his followers.

Stippling and frosting was used from time to time to give variety to the clear glass. The charm of the group of ribbon patterns is due to this contrast of clear and frosted surfaces. Ribbon patterns were stripe patterns with alternating frosted and clear glass. These patterns were first made by Bakewell, Pears & Company after 1850. Compotes are particularly attractive and available in the ribbon patterns. These patterns are related to the later frosted group, but the frosted surface on the earlier patterns is rough to the touch, while that on the later Lion, Westward Ho, Three Face, Jumbo, and others is smooth. Gillinder & Sons of Philadelphia produced the Westward Ho, Lion, and Classic patterns soon after the Centennial in 1876, and the majority of the other frosted patterns were made between then and 1885. These patterns are popular with collectors for their interesting shapes, for the decorative finials on the covers of compotes and other dishes, and for the attractive scenes on goblets, plates and other flat surface pieces. The figures on the covers and the bands including the scenes were frosted. The figure of a Kneeling Indian is on the Westward Ho finial and the scenes include a log cabin in the mountains, bison running on the plains and deer. The Lion pattern has finials of a head or figure of a lion and the stems of compotes and vases have lion heads. The platter and bread plate have a panel with a raised scene of one or two lions. Another attractive frosted pattern is the Deer and Dog. The frosted dog stands on the top of the covered dishes and a frosted scene of running deer is shown in panels on the body of the pieces. Westward Ho, Lion, and Three Face are among the most popular pressed glass patterns today so it follows that they are expensive. Other less popular frosted patterns might be a better bet for the beginning collector.

Another large group of pattern glass includes the Dewdrop and Hobnail patterns and their many variations. Dewdrop patterns began to be made in the 1860's. The earliest and one of the most pleasing of the group is the Dewdrop with Star. It is covered with small pointed dots known as dewdrops and in the center of the plates and many other pieces the dewdrops form a star. This pattern is brilliant and decorative and deservedly popular. It is made in many different pieces, but some plates and other pieces have been reproduced. Other variants of the Dewdrop include Panelled Dewdrop, Popcorn, and the later patterns such as Dew and Raindrop, Beaded Dewdrop, Beaded Loop, 101, and many others.

The Hobnail patterns also form a large group. The early Pointed Hobnail is clear and brilliant. One style has a heavy thumbnail base and another has ball feet. Pointed Hobnail was made in amber and blue as well as clear glass and in rare apple and dark green, and yellow. There are attractive footed cake plates and berry bowls with pointed edges and with fan top. The later Hobnail patterns have flattened hobs. There is also a Panelled Hobnail pattern made in yellow, blue, amber, and opaque white as well as clear glass and there are four types of opalescent hobnail in yellow and blue colorings. In the 1860's a group of clear conventional patterns was also made. These included Buckle, Diamond, Chain and Shield, Barley, and Cape Cod.

A group of mythological patterns included Cupid and Venus, Psyche and Cupid, and Minerva. Then there is the well-known Deer and Pine Tree which was made in amber, blue, yellow, and apple green as well as white, and the interesting Hand pattern with a clutching hand on the tops of covered dishes. The Centennial or Liberty Bell was also made at this time. The plates have a bell in their centers and the dates 1776–1876, the patent date September 28, 1875 and the inscription "100 Years Ago." The oval platters have the names of all the signers of the Declaration with a large Liberty Bell in the center. Most of this glass was made by Gillinder & Sons. Needless to say, this pattern is in demand and though available, is not inexpensive.

The flower and fruit groups were favorites in the 1860's and 1880's when they were made and they are some of the best known and most popular with collectors today. The majority of these patterns were partly stippled and were made in colored as well as clear glass. The patterns include many sentimental Victorian flowers such as roses, fuchsias, lilies of the valley, forget-me-nots, and bleeding hearts. Rose in Snow, which is the best known of the various rose patterns, is a favorite with collectors. It is a delightful pattern which is found not only in clear glass, but in blue, amber, and yellow. Some pieces such as plates and goblets have been reproduced. The covered pieces with clear stems and finials are especially attractive and there is a small mug with handles and the inscription, "In Fond Remembrance." Other favorite patterns are Rose Sprig, Wildflower, and Primrose. Among the berry or leaf patterns, Barberry is the most popular and since it was made in great quantities by many factories it is not hard to find. Other attractive patterns in this group are Blackberry, Currant, Strawberry, and the Baltimore Pear. Later stippled patterns include the Princess Feather, Anthemion, Shell and Tassel, Fish Scale, Roman Rosette, and Picket which was made in the 1890's.

Colored pressed glass is especially popular with many collectors and among the most sought-after patterns today is Thousand Eye which was made in yellow, blue, apple green, amber, clear glass and rare opalescent. There were also several red and white glass combina-

Carnival Glass. LEFT. Corn and Husk vase. RIGHT. Thistle design pitcher. (*Rose M. Presznick*)

tions such as Ruby Thumbprint, and Red Block which are late patterns of the '90's. There is also the Ribbed Opal, Emerald Green, a group of Fine Cut patterns, Cane and Basket Weave patterns, which are all made in the colored as well as clear glass. Among the late patterns of the 1880's the best known and most popular was the attractive Daisy and Button with its many variants. These patterns were made in the many articles of tableware, but also in novelties such as hats, shoes, umbrellas, animals, birds, cornucopias and kettles, some of which were for use as match safes and toothpick holders.

This brief outline only suggests a few of the many patterns and articles available to the collector of Victorian Pressed Glass. A few guideposts for collectors might be helpful. In forming a collection of any kind, it is always more interesting to specialize. Also, a collection of any one object or any one pattern of glass is more valuable than odd pieces. A complete table setting of a pressed glass pattern although sometimes difficult to assemble is delightful to own. If the collector is working with a limited budget such pieces as goblets are a good item to collect. Also such articles as toothpick holders, match safes, and other small novelties are comparatively inexpensive and make an interesting display. The most expensive patterns are Westward Ho, Three Faces, and Lion in that order. These are desirable because of their popularity and unique design.

One of the most interesting categories of pressed glass collecting would be plates and platters with American historical significance. Beginning with the Centennial bread plate and platter made by Gillinder & Sons, these commemorative plates with mottos, flags, eagles, portraits and scenery were made down until the time of the World's Columbian Exposition in 1893. They include plates with portraits of Washington, Garfield, Grant, Cleveland and Hendricks, and McKinley. The Washington plates were made by Gillinder & Sons and some had center medallions of Independence Hall, while others depicted Carpenters' Hall where the Continental Congress first assembled. Bread plates or platters, with the Sheaf of Wheat centers, Liberty Bell, or Bunker Hill

Monument, Horseshoe, and a Grape Pattern plate inscribed, "It is Pleasant To Labor For Those We Love," are also interesting collector's pieces. Another commemorative platter is the Railroad platter made by the Bellaire Goblet Company of Findlay, Ohio, to commemorate the opening of the Union Pacific Railroad in 1869. The Knights of Labor platter with steamship and train was made by the United States Glass Company of Pittsburgh. A round tray to hold pitcher and glasses has a center Currier & Ives darky scene and there is a bread plate with grape border and The Last Supper after Leonardo da Vinci in the center. A large attractive tray depicting Niagara Falls was made by Adams & Co. of Pittsburgh in the 1870's. All these pieces are unique and interesting for a historical collection although they are not as attractive as some of the other patterns.

It takes study and experience and familiarity to recognize authentic old pressed glass. The clear ring does not necessarily mean the glass is

Goblets, late bird patterns. LEFT. Hummingbird. CENTER. Flamingo. RIGHT. Cardinal. (*The Bennington Museum, Bennington, Vermont;* PHOTO. *Lloyd Studio*)

nineteenth century. It does mean it is good quality glass. Colored glass will not ring as clear as clear glass, for most colored glass is late glass and not as good quality. However, collectors are not as interested in glass quality as glass pattern, or Daisy and Button, which is not top quality glass, would not be as popular as it is. If you are a beginning collector start your collection with a piece from an authorized glass dealer. Even though you may pay more you can be sure you have a good piece and you can learn much from him before you start to pick up odd pieces at the flea market. So much pressed glass has been reproduced that it is important to watch for copies in certain pieces such as plates, goblets, and sugars and creamers. In reproductions color usually varies and even clear glass may look dull. Also the details of the patterns are often lacking. Although cracked or nicked pieces are sold it is better to have a perfect piece of an unknown pattern than a cracked piece of one of the more popular patterns unless it is a particularly rare item. Also, it is best to start with a pattern that is not too popular such as the late but attractive Herringbone which combines herringbone panels with loops and diamonds filled with dewdrops. Since this design is not too well known it is not in demand and thus the prices are more reasonable, and a clear glass Herringbone covered sugar, footed sugar, and creamer are an attractive addition to any table. The shapes of pieces of pressed glass are a means of dating them, as are the articles made. Early shapes were more graceful while later shapes were bulky and often low-slung in outline. While the sugar and creamer, spoon holder, and butter dish were found in the early sets of pressed glass such pieces as the caster and the syrup jug did not appear until late in the century.

Covered Animal Dishes

ONE of the favorite items with collectors today is the covered pressed glass animal dish. These were made in opaque glass, mostly white, but some were made in blue and combinations of blue and white, and some were made in black glass. Hens and roosters were made in the greatest quantity, but there were also cats, dogs, lambs, fish, horses, bears, rabbits, cows, eagles, lions, elephants, bears, swans, quail and many other animals. There is also a cover with the battleship *Maine* and several with the bust of Admiral Dewey.

Animal dishes were made by many glass factories in the 1880's including M'Kee Bros. of Pittsburgh; Westmoreland Glass Company; Challinor, Taylor & Co.; United States Glass Co.; Central Glass Co.; and Indiana Tumbler & Goblet Co. Many companies advertised farmyard groups which included fish, ducks, swans, hens, roosters and eagles. The farmyard groups of both Challinor, Taylor & Co. and United States Glass Co. were made in opal, turquoise and olive, and were made both with and without glass eyes. There are varying details of bases on the dishes; some have basket bases, others have a pattern of cattails and pond lilies and others have fluted or diamond all-over patterns. The details and workmanship on the Atterbury and M'Kee animal dishes are usually superior to that of other manufacturers. Many of these dishes were patented. The famous Atterbury ducks were patented in 1887 by the Atterbury Company of Pittsburgh, Pennsylvania. They were made in white, blue, black or amethyst, and in many color combinations such as white with a blue head. The ducks had a pressed design of conventional feathers and glass eyes. They are marked on the base with the patent date and are rare. There were other ducks made by Challinor, Taylor & Company and by other glass companies. Also, the Atterbury duck has been reproduced without the patent date.

Hens are the most popular animal dishes because there are more of them available since they were made in vast quantities and distributed as premiums. There were many types of hens, some with heads facing front and others with heads turned. There were also various types of bases: rib pattern, basket weave, and lacy edge. The hens and roosters with basket bases edged with a chain border were shown in the Challinor, Taylor & Company catalogue, and similar large hen and rooster dishes were made by the United States Glass Co. who took over their line. A hen with a base showing small chicks was made by Flaccus Company of Wheeling, West Virginia, who used ornate bases on all of their animal dishes. Hens on ribbed bases were usually made by M'Kee Bros. A hen on a lacy edge base was made by Atterbury as was the rare chick and eggs on a lacy base. Atterbury hens were made in various colors of marble, blue, brown, green and yellow and plain colors with blue, amber and amethyst heads. Lacy edged dishes with fox, lion, fish, hand and dove, cat, and swan were also made by Atterbury. The swan dish has been reproduced by Westmoreland Glass Company. M'Kee made a swan on a ribbed base and other M'Kee animals on ribbed bases include dove, duck, turkey, cow, rabbit, squirrel and lion. These are found marked and unmarked. All of these are rare and scarce. M'Kee dishes are usually found in milk-white glass. Some are marked on the inside of the cover. Later, these dishes were made by the Indiana Tumbler and Goblet Co. in Greentown, Indiana.

Covered Dishes. Opaque white pressed glass fish, dog, cat. Opaque blue rooster. Green clear glass rabbit. (*The Henry Ford Museum*)

Animal dishes were sometimes painted with gold and naturalistic colors. The rare Indiana Tumbler and Goblet Co. robin on a nest is often found with remnants of paint. A similar robin was also made by Vallerystahl and reproduced by Westmoreland Glass Company. The head turns down instead of up and the base is a design of reeds. So many dishes, including the hens and turkey dishes, have been reproduced both by Westmoreland and Vallerystahl in France that one has to be careful when buying these dishes. Also, many dishes are found fitted to bases other than those originally made for them. Sometimes it is easy to spot the wrong base, but if a base fits it may be difficult to know whether or not it is original. Generally speaking, lacy-edge and split rib bases are old, and basket bases have been more often reproduced. The highly decorative story-telling Flaccus bases are particularly interesting although Flaccus dishes are not as good in design and workmanship as those made by Atterbury and M'Kee.

Glass Novelties

THE Victorians loved souvenirs. They bought silver spoons with scenes and names of the cities they visited. They brought back souvenir shells painted or engraved with "Atlantic City"; pitchers inscribed "Niagara Falls," and painted with a scene of the Falls; and red and white glass was marked "Mother," "Father," or "World's Columbian Exposition, Chicago 1893." But some of the most popular souvenirs were the pressed glass novelties made from the 1870's to the end of the century.

The fad probably started at the Philadelphia Centennial where many small pressed glass objects were given away by glass companies at their booths. Other glass souvenirs could be purchased. These souvenirs included such objects as toothpick and match holders, mustard jars, horse radish dishes, and baskets to hold flowers as favors on the dining table. They were made in such shapes as umbrellas, chairs, cradles, wheelbarrows, hands, coal hods, tree trunks and fans, as well as hats, slippers and shoes.

These souvenirs were made by many of the glass companies working in America at this time, but the majority were made by the following companies; Bryce Bros.; King Glass Co.; Gillinder & Sons; Central Glass Co.; Doyle & Co.; Adams & Co.; Bellaire Goblet Co.; Phoenix Glass Co.; and U. S. Glass Co., which later absorbed many of the other companies.

Most of the glass novelties were made in Daisy and Button pattern, some were made in Cube pattern, and others were pressed in wicker or brick patterns. Although some novelties have been found only in clear glass the majority of the pieces were made in amber, blue and crystal, and a few were made in marble glass.

One of the best-known toothpick or match holders was the Kitten on a Cushion with a Daisy and Button cup. It was made in aquamarine blue, amber, and crystal. There was also a dog holding a cornucopia vase, a rooster beside a toothpick holder, a rabbit holding a vase, and a holder with a baby chick. A bird beside a basket was made by Bryce Bros. A rare Daisy and Button cradle was made in clear glass and in amber. A unique corset toothpick holder was made by Bellaire Goblet Co. The clock match safe in Daisy and Button pattern was also made by Bellaire.

Glass novelties in Daisy and Button, Cube, and Wicker patterns. Blue, amber, crystal. (*The New-York Historical Society*)

Glass hats and boots, shoes, and slippers have long been favorite items with collectors. They were also favorites of the glass blowers in the old glass houses who usually made them out of leftover glass for their own amusement. For this reason they were one of a kind pieces and thus rare. Early hats were blown into bottle molds. Some show patterns of thumbprint and ribbing and swirling. There are also hats in all the different types of Victorian Art Glass including Burmese, Spatter, cased glass, and striped glass made by Nicholas Lutz at Sandwich. Needless to say, these are rare and expensive. There were also many souvenir hats made for exhibitions and World's Fairs, and also some hats were made for advertising novelties.

Hats were made in Hobnail and Fine Rib pattern pressed glass. But the hats made late in the nineteenth century in such patterns as Cube, Raindrop, Thousand Eye, Daisy and Star, and Daisy and Button are the ones available to the average collector. The largest variety are to be found in Daisy and Button. Some are made in clear glass with blue or red buttons or hat bands. The Daisy and Button hat toothpick holder was made in clear, blue, amber, canary yellow, amethyst and smoke, with various combinations of colors in the buttons and hat bands. There were also larger hats in Daisy and Button pattern which were designed as spoon holders or celery vases.

Bottles and drinking glasses were blown in the shape of boots. Victorian glass makers were more interested in the ladies' shoe and slipper, and the pressed glass Daisy and Button pattern was made in styles of existing Victorian shoes. There were high button shoes, low laced slippers, and slippers with buckles and bows. These were made as holders for toilet water bottles, pincushions, and salt and pepper shakers. A slipper mounted on a tray was made by Bryce Bros. as an ash tray. It was made in blue, amber, yellow, and crystal. A Daisy and Button slipper on skates was made by United States Glass Co. There is also a Diamond Block pattern slipper on skates. It was made in blue, crystal, and other colors. A slipper in a metal holder is often marked "Gillinder & Sons Centennial Exhibition." It was made in crystal, frosted and milk-white glass in various sizes. A Puss in Boots slipper was made by Bryce Bros. and is a familiar favorite of collectors. It has been reproduced. There were many slippers in Cane and Fine Cut patterns.

Slippers were made in greater quantity than other types of shoes and are therefore more plentiful today. Pressed glass slippers are the easiest to find, but there were also slippers made in milk glass, spatter, marble, and Bristol type as well as other kinds of art glass slippers with painted decorations which were made at Sandwich and New England Glass Company. These are very rare. Shoes of marble glass and black opaque glass are rare and a high glass boot with a spur is also rare. Glass novelties and hats and shoes have been reproduced.

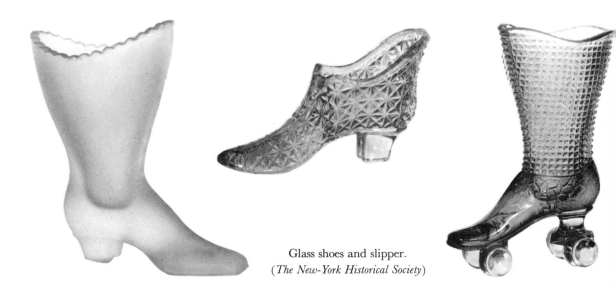

Glass shoes and slipper.
(*The New-York Historical Society*)

Cut Glass

COLLECTORS have been so absorbed in collecting Victorian Pressed Glass and Fancy Art Glass that American cut glass has not only been neglected but scorned, and if one happened to own a piece it was not thought worth keeping. The reason for this scorn and neglect lies partly in the fact that little was known about this glass and the present day popularity of cut glass is to a certain extent due to the information given for collectors in Dorothy Daniel's book, *Cut and Engraved Glass*, the first book in the field. The classification of patterns and glass houses gives the collector definite information on which to start a collection.

There are three periods of American cut glass beginning with the glass cut at Stiegel glassworks in Pennsylvania from 1771. This Early American cut glass continued to be made until 1830 when methods of manufacture changed. The commercial output after this date and especially that of the late Brilliant Period 1880–1905, is the glass which concerns collectors of Victorian cut glass. The glass of the Middle Period is characterized by flute cuttings. Heavy flute-cut compotes, pitchers and decanters with diamond-cut bands, fluted neck rings or panel cutting with heavy steeple or mushroom stoppers were in use on every well-appointed table. This flute-cut glass was made by many glass houses, particularly in Pennsylvania and West Virginia. As the period progressed, more pieces were made and there are flute-cut goblets, champagne glasses, spoon holders, celery vases and bowls made between 1830 and 1845. Attractive celery vases with petal tops and fluted glasses with cutting on their feet were made by Sweeney Glass Company, Wheeling, West Virginia, in the 1840's. Some of these middle period pieces were cut in floral patterns and decorated with engraving. Colored, flashed, and cased glass was also made at this time. The red and crystal glass cut with stars, prisms, and diamonds, as well as blue and green glass made at New England Glass Company and by Dorflinger was especially popular. Other glass with color was made by Hobbs, Barnes & Company of Wheeling, West Virginia, and by Mulvaney and Ledlie

LEFT. Ribbon Star pattern cut glass, Libbey Glass Co., 1890–1893. RIGHT. Butterfly and Primrose plate, intaglio cutting. (*American Cut Glass for the Discriminating Collector* by J. Michael and Dorothy T. Pearson)

at Pittsburgh. The cut glass industry grew profitably until the craze for pressed glass crowded many of the manufacturers of the most expensive blown and cut glass products out of business. But in 1876 the exhibits of cut glass at the Philadelphia Centennial again created a demand for cut glass.

The glass of this later period is distinguished for its fine-line cutting which became known as brilliant cutting. This glass is heavy and crystal clear and is characterized by deep curved miter cuttings called splits, and such design motifs as hob-star, notched prism, and fan. Cut glass could now be bought in table settings, including goblets, wines, champagnes, sherry and claret glasses, plates, ice cream dishes, finger bowls, butter pats, salts and peppers, compotes, bonbon dishes, nappies, pickle and celery dishes, berry bowls, punch cups, flower vases and candlesticks. All of these various cut glass pieces were made in thousands of patterns by all the well-known glass houses of the period. The important glass houses that made cut glass were C. Dorflinger & Sons, White Mills, Pennsylvania; Gillinder & Sons, Philadelphia, Pa.; T. G. Hawkes Glass Company, Corning, New York; the United States Glass Company, Tiffin, Ohio; Libbey Glass Company, Toledo, Ohio; Pairpoint Corporation, New Bedford, Massachusetts; and H. C. Fry Glass Company, Rochester, Pa.

Glass of the Brilliant Period is easily recognized. It is deeper cut than the earlier cut glass and the cuttings are more intricate and elaborate. New cuttings such as Curved Split, Prism, Chair Bottom, and Hob-Star are combined with older simpler motifs such as Hobnail, Fan, Block, Bull's Eye, and Strawberry-Diamond. There are about fifty documented patterns available to the collector today. The earlier patterns such as Russian, Middlesex, Parisian, Strawberry-Diamond and Fan are clearly defined. Later the patterns were more ornate and have several decorative motifs in one pattern such as Star or Pin Wheel with Prism or Bull's Eye motifs so that it is more difficult to recognize the pattern. Also each pattern had many variations. Probably the best-

Cut glass plate, Russian pattern by T. G. Hawkes & Co. (*The Corning Museum of Glass*)

known pattern of Brilliant Period cut glass is the Russian. This pattern was patented for T. G. Hawkes Glass Company, but was also made by C. Dorflinger & Sons. Russian pattern was first made for the Russian Embassy in Washington. It was also made for the American Embassy in St. Petersburg and for the White House in Washington in 1886. The Russian pattern is a refinement of the old Star and Hobnail and consists of borders of various sizes of stars alternating with hobnails and has a large center star. Another favorite pattern with collectors is the Parisian pattern. It was made by C. Dorflinger & Sons from 1886. It is a simple pattern of Curved Splits, Fans, and Strawberry-Diamond crosshatchings. Pieces have a star bottom. The Middlesex is a pattern made up of the eight-point star motif. It was made at the New England Glass Company and is especially attractive and rare. Grecian is another rare pattern which is of interest to collectors. It has a field of fine star and hobnail cutting with lozenge-shaped ovals of clear glass.

Strawberry-Diamond and Fan is a fairly common pattern and is

LEFT. Cut glass pitcher, C. Dorflinger & Sons, 1897. (*Brooklyn Museum*) RIGHT. Rose bowl on standard, Brunswick pattern. (*J. Michael and Dorothy T. Pearson*)

easily recognized and also easy to find today. It was also less expensive and thus more popular when made than the more ornate combinations of stars, although the finest pieces can be identified by a 24 point star in the center. This pattern was made by T. G. Hawkes Glass Company, Libby Glass Company, J. Hoare & Company and many others. It was cut in red, green, and yellow as well as clear glass. Other patterns that are fairly easy to identify and good collectors' items because there were quantities made by the many glass houses, were Princess, a pattern with strawberry-diamond points and fan scallops with hob-star center motif; Harvard, a so-called chair bottom pattern of raised squares with alternate squares crosshatched; and Corinthian which has a 16 point hob-star as its center motif within a Greek cross—decorated by cross-hatching. This pattern was cut by nearly every glass house.

Late in the century cut glass patterns became more intricate and confused. The simple star became a pinwheel or buzz which was a many-pointed swirling star with swirled fan-cuts at the star points. Variations of the pattern were also made. Realistic floral patterns such as Bristol Rose, Lily of the Valley, Cornflower and fruit patterns and combinations of cutting and engraving were made at the end of the period. These patterns were made at the end of the century and the designs are realistic, with none of the old cut glass star or rosette motifs.

Brilliant Period cut glass can be identified by pattern, the weight of the glass, and by trade-mark. However, since the same patterns were made by many glass houses these do not seem good criteria for identification. Many, but certainly not all, pieces of glass were marked with an acid or pressed stamp and this is a definite means of identification, but lack of a mark does not mean that it is not good quality glass. The best way to identify cut glass is to study the finer specimens of the pattern which you choose to collect. Also, it helps to handle pieces. All good cut glass is heavy and the edges should be sharp to the touch. When a piece is held to the light there is refraction. The edges of a motif should appear sharply defined. Every piece should be examined in a bright light. Carry a magnifying glass and look for chips or other flaws in cutting.

Cut glass vase, C. Dorflinger & Sons, 1897. (*Brooklyn Museum*)

Buy only perfect pieces and if your budget is limited collect small pieces. Rose bowls, baskets, finger bowls, candlesticks, water glasses and wine glasses make attractive items for the collector. Also, there are many small articles of cut glass such as cruets, cologne and smelling salts bottles, covered powder boxes, pin trays, salt and pepper shakers, toothpick holders, knife rests and butter pats which should interest the collector of small inexpensive articles.

Cut glass was never cheap but it is the one "antique" which sells for less today than when it was made. Cut glass varies in price according to locality and demand. Generally it is more expensive in city than in country antique shops. Good places to look for cut glass are West Virginia, northeastern Pennsylvania and Ohio, where so many of the glass houses were located. One advantage to collecting cut glass is the fact that it has seldom been reproduced and because of the cost of hand labor and the few glass cutters working today, cut glass probably never will be reproduced.

Paperweights

ALTHOUGH the techniques used in making paperweights go back to ancient craftsmen and to the latticino glass made at the Venetian glass houses in the Renaissance, paperweights as we know them are essentially a product of Victorian times. The first dated weights were made in St. Louis, France, in the 1840's and were introduced to American glasshouses soon afterward by François Pierre and Nicholas Lutz who had been trained in France. However, the most popular period for paperweights was between 1860 and 1875. Although the best American paperweights were made at the New England Glass Company by François Pierre and at the Sandwich Glass Company by Nicholas Lutz, fine paperweights were also made by John L. Gilliland in Brooklyn and at Mount Washington Glass Works in South Boston, and from 1863 to 1912 by Whitall, Tatum & Company at Millville, New Jersey. Some paperweights were made by practically all of the large flint glass houses.

LEFT. Paperweight with canes and latticino background. (*The Corning Museum of Glass*) RIGHT. Paperweight by Ralph Barber, Millville, New Jersey, c. 1900. (*The Henry Ford Museum*)

The techniques of American paperweights followed the French. There were millefiori weights with rods of conventional flower patterns and there were designs which incorporated fruits and flowers. There were also cameos or "sulphides" encrusted in glass. Some weights are further enhanced by cutting and faceting and some are made of overlay or case glass in several colors. Most paperweights are built, not blown. Millefiori weights are made of pieces of glass cane cut into short lengths. These pieces are arranged in patterns face down on a mold. When the design is completed the background of white latticino is put in, then both design and background are encased in the clear glass dome through a process of heating. Then the weight is smoothed and polished. Sulphides and other items are similarly set in place and then encased in the glass dome.

Many millefiori or candy type weights were made at Sandwich Glass Company. They also made fruit and flower designs including the dahlia, pansy, fuchsia, and the well-known Christmas poinsettia. The strawberry weight was created by Nicholas Lutz who specialized in fruit weights that show tiny apples, cherries, or pears with green leaves against a white latticino background. The majority of the paperweights made at the New England Glass Company were also of millefiori glass, but they were best known for the large apples and pears. These were

LEFT. Boston & Sandwich Glass Company. Pink dahlia with green leaves. (C. W. Lyon) RIGHT. Boston & Sandwich Glass Company. Flower with rose stripes. (*The Corning Museum of Glass*)

blown from tubes of glass. When the fruit was blown it was fastened to the glass base by heat. After the Civil War this factory made a weight in the form of a black and white English bulldog, and green glass turtle weights. A late souvenir weight in the form of Plymouth Rock was also made. A rare sulphide of Queen Victoria and Prince Albert was made in the 1850's. John L. Gilliland made fine millefiori weights, some with faceted cutting on the crown and sides which frame the tiny pink, green, and white flowers. The Mount Washington Glass Company is known for a beautiful red aster set on green leaves, and for a frilled pink rose with leaves and two buds.

LEFT. Orange and yellow pear on clear glass base. New England Glass Company. (*The Henry Ford Museum*) RIGHT. Blown glass apple on clear base. New England Glass Company. (*The Corning Museum of Glass*)

The best-known rose, however, was the Millville Rose made by Whitall, Tatum & Company, from 1863. These roses were made in deep rose pink, yellow, and white both with and without stems. The rose is usually upright and rests on a cylinder base or on a baluster stem. This is a late weight made by Ralph Barber between 1905 and 1912. Millville also made a lily weight and one called Devil's Fire. There were also weights showing a hunter and his dog and weights with eagles, horses, sailboats, and flowers in pots. These weights are attributed to Michael Kane and although inferior in craftsmanship are interesting examples of truly American paperweights and are related to American primitive art.

Paperweights were also made by Pairpont Manufacturing Company who made a beautiful red and blue spiral twist set on a pedestal with engraving on top and base; at Dorflinger in Pennsylvania; at the Clyde Glass Works in Clyde, New York; at the Ravenna Glass Works in Ravenna, Ohio; at White Glass Works in Zanesville, Ohio, and at many other midwestern glass houses. About 1890 Ravenna Glass Company made a white lily with bubble leaves. A similar lily, but red, set in a ground of sparkling vari-colored glass is a modern weight made by Ravenna. Crude paper weights of bottle glass were made at Redford Glass Works, Plattsburg, New York, and the Redwood Glass Works, Watertown. Some had an Indian Head cent imbedded in the glass. There were also weights enclosing decals and porcelain plaques.

Late in the century popular sentimental weights were made with inscriptions such as "Remember Me," "Friendship," "From a Friend" and "Home Sweet Home." These were accompanied by floral sprays or clasped hands. There were also paperweights with patriotic symbols and Masonic symbols. The popular Three Little Pigs weight was made at Somerville Glass Company in Massachusetts. The designs in these are usually white against the clear glass. There were also faceted clear cut glass weights. Tiffany made a weight of sea urchins and waves and in the early 1900's he also made a paperweight doorstop in blue and green Favrile glass. It is signed "L. C. Tiffany Favrile." A door knob had cameo busts of Monroe and Harrison encrusted in deep blue glass. Other weights had cameos of Washington and Lincoln. Tiny glass buttons containing roses were made at Sandwich, and footed inkwells with tall pointed stoppers were made at Millville.

Modern paperweights are still being made in America as well as in France, Sweden, Scotland, and Japan. Most of the modern weights, such as the sulphide zodiac series by Baccarat and the Swedish Kosta Glass Works, Hammarskjold weights are original modern weights, but those made in Japan are often copies of nineteenth century millefiori designs and are passed as old by some dealers. The red lily Ravenna weight and the perfume bottle with the pink rose resembling the Millville rose are also sometimes sold as old weights. Modern weights when sold as modern are worth collecting, but because they are being made one must have some criteria for the valuation of old weights. First of all, old weights are heavier. Old paper weights may have smooth bottoms, but they were never frosted. American weights are seldom marked so they must be judged by workmanship, color, and design. It is not difficult to learn the designs of American weights because the most of them are uniquely American, but it is difficult to attribute a certain weight to a definite glass house. For example, all New England glass companies made millefiori weights, and New England Glass Company, Sandwich, and Mount Washington were at one time controlled by the same man; thus both designs and workmen may have been interchangeable. Paperweights made in Japan have harsh chemical coloring. It is, of course, best to buy a paperweight in good condi-

Millville Rose, Whitall, Tatum & Co.
(*C. W. Lyon*)

Paperweight. South Jersey, c. 1900.
(*The Henry Ford Museum*)

tion, but scratches and even chips can be smoothed and polished, and if the weight is authentic it is well worth the price of repair.

Art Glass

IN the last quarter of the nineteenth century American glasshouses began to produce the hand-blown, hand-decorated glass which we call Art Glass. All known techniques were used and many new ones invented by talented men such as Nicholas Lutz, Frederick Carder, and Louis C. Tiffany. The dominant characteristic of Victorian Art Glass is its color, which varied from brilliant clear glass to delicate pastels. Texture was also an interesting feature. It ranged from sandpaper effects such as that of Tree of Life to the satiny smoothness of Satin Glass. Shaded effects were produced by reheating with gold; glass was made to look like silver; and a smooth finish was obtained with a bath of hydrofluoric acid or a sanding process.

Patterns striking or subtle were made by molding, by applied glass decoration, or by enamel painting. Such patterns as hobnails, swirls, and diamond quilt were molded; applied decoration was added by the glass blower after the form was made; and enamel decoration such as flowers, leaves, and Mary Gregory designs were painted after the article was fired. Many of the forms of Art Glass are graceful and dignified, others are frilled, crimped, and fancy. To cover fully the different types of Victorian Art Glass requires a book. In this short résumé the various kinds of glass will be grouped according to their techniques.

In the group of shaded glass, Peachblow was one of the most popular. The Peachblow made by Hobbs, Brockunier & Company at Wheeling is clear and has a milk white lining. In coloring it is a deep red shading to greenish yellow and in its velvety finish it resembles Chinese porcelain. Several different glass houses made Peachblow and the products of each company vary in color and also in trade name. The Peachblow made at Mount Washington and New England Glass Company was a homogeneous opaque glass. That at New England Glass Company shades from ivory to tints of deep rose. It was called

Wild Rose. Agate is a variation of Peachblow with a mottled effect. Mount Washington Peachblow is more delicate and shades from shell-pink to light blue. Burmese was another type of shaded glass. It, however, was made by only one factory, Mount Washington at New Bedford, Massachusetts, in both dull and glossy finish in a variety of forms, including tablewares. The colors range from greenish yellow to delicate pink and the decoration was molded, applied or painted. Molded patterns include hobnail and diamond, and painted designs range from grasses and butterflies of Japanese inspiration to Egyptian motifs.

Amberina was produced at Mount Washington and at the New England Glass Company. Its deep red and yellow colorings are similar to Wheeling Peachblow. Amberina was made in both table and ornamental wares in patterns of thumbprint, ribbing, and expanded diamonds.

Royal Flemish and Crown Milano are also included in the category of shaded glass. Both have colorings of beige and rust and are enamelled with oriental patterns. The designs of Royal Flemish are outlined in gold on the mat ground which varies from beige to russet tones. The flowers and maple leaves of Crown Milano are enameled and gilt on a light creamy ground.

Another type of glass which caught the fancy of the Victorian public was a glass which combined different colors of glass in a confetti-like effect. It went by the general name of spatter or spangle, but certain types such as Tortoise Shell combined browns and tans in a manner which imitated real tortoise shell, and others imitated a moss agate. Spangled glass was a novelty glass which originated at Hobbs, Brockunier & Company in 1883. The finished glass form was rolled in mica and then returned to the furnace. Vasa Murrhina was a variation of Spangled Glass. It was made at Sandwich, and at the Vasa Murrhina Art Glass Company.

Frosted glass was another popular type of Victorian Art Glass. These wares have an interesting textured surface. Pomona glass, which originated at the New England Glass Company, is a delicate clear glass stained with pale amber color and decorated with pale blue flowers and straw-color leaves. Tree of Life is a pressed glass pattern

Wheeling Peachblow vase with tall stem. Small vase, cream with looped design of amber and green. Emil J. Larsen, Vineland, N. J. (*The Henry Ford Museum*)

BELOW. Amberina-Peachblow-Burmese. LEFT TO RIGHT. Amberina trumpet vase, New England Glass Co., Amberina diamond-quilted footed bowl, Sandwich; Amberina toothpick holder, New England Glass Co.; Jack-in-the-Pulpit, "Mt. Washington" Peachblow vase, rose shading to palest blue, Mt. Washington Glass Co.; Satin Burmese Hobnail sugar and creamer, salmon shading to lemon. Mt. Washington Glass Co., New Bedford; fluted bowl, Peachblow, rose shading to cream-white. New England Glass Co., Cambridge, Mass. (*The Chrysler Art Museum of Provincetown*)

first copyrighted by the Portland Glass Company in 1869. It was afterwards made at other companies and is found in both clear and colored tableware, baskets, bottles, and more ornate shapes such as the epergne encircled with a clear red glass snake. Overshot glass is a rough frosted glass covered with bits of crushed glass which were blown into the hot glass. It is sometimes decorated with applied flower decoration. Effects of crackling were produced by blowing the glass into a mold. It was made in several colors.

Pearl wares were made by varying the glass with acid or sand to give it a satiny finish. These pearl wares are of several types, but Mother-of-Pearl and Satin Glass are best known. The majority of the pearl wares have a white lining and a colored coating. Mother-of-Pearl is the most elaborate. It is made up of several layers of glass and distinguished by the patterns of diamonds, swirls, and herringbone. The beauty of this glass is in the beautiful coloring of blues, pinks, oranges and canary yellow. The rarest colors are robin's egg blue, bittersweet, and rainbow.

Plain Satin Glass without decoration or pattern was made in similar colors. It was also made in swirl patterns, with applied decoration such as flowers and leaves, and often glass beads were added. Satin

Group of spatter and spangled glass. LEFT TO RIGHT. "Vasa Murrhina" vase, Boston and Sandwich Glass Co.; "Vasa Murrhina" pitcher, Boston and Sandwich Glass Co.; "Agata" stick vase. New England Glass Co.; Rainbow Spangled vase, Boston and Sandwich Glass Co.; enameled "Tortoise Shell" basket, Sandwich. (*The Chrysler Art Museum of Provincetown*)

Three Sandwich epergnes. LEFT TO RIGHT. Yellow opaque and clear epergne; cranberry and clear epergne; "Tree-of-Life," clear with red snake and gilding. (*The Chrysler Art Museum of Provincetown*)

glass with a bead pattern of coral, seaweed or wheat is called Coralene.

Opalescent glass was made in pressed glass, pattern glass and blown and molded glass. Some pieces are opalescent throughout such as onyx, others have clear or colored glass borders, and some have combination effects such as striped Swirl and Dewdrop. The opalescence is made by manipulation of the various glass mixtures. Spanish Lace and Onyx patterns with their delicate floral patterns and the various Swirl combinations are the most interesting.

Opaque glass was made in pressed tablewares and also in fancy novelty shapes. The best known opaque is white Milk Glass. Opaque glass was made at Sandwich, and at New England Glass Company in the first third of the nineteenth century as lamp bases and candlesticks, vases, and such individual pieces as salts. Later tableware patterns such as Wheat Panel, Ribbed Grape, Blackberry, Almond, Thumbprint, Sawtooth, Flower and Panel, and Lincoln Drape were made in opaque

LEFT TO RIGHT. Overshot vases c. 1875, clear and opaque with applied multicolor decoration of fruit and flowers. Blue overshot; clear pale blue, attached amber rim and feet; white cased with pink, attached bright blue rim and feet; clear cranberry, but opalescent at rim and bottom, attached pale green handle. Boston and Sandwich Glass Co. (*The Chrysler Art Museum of Provincetown*)

LEFT TO RIGHT. Overshot vase. Opaque pink encrusted with clear glass, applied clear glass feet; sapphire blue vase with white enameled Mary Gregory decoration. Boston and Sandwich Glass Co.; Amberina vase with applied handles. (*The Henry Ford Museum*)

pressed glass and also many openwork plates, bowls and compotes intended for dessert were made.

There are a hundred or more patterns of milk glass plates: lacy-edged, flower, bird, historical, children's plates and comic plates as well as geometric designs were made in opaque white, black, blue, amethyst and a rare chartreuse green. Many of the patterns were pressed, but others were painted with bird and flower designs. These plates with their various types of decorative lacy borders are popular with collectors today. They were made down into the twentieth century, as witness the William Jennings Bryan plate.

Milk Glass lamps and candlesticks were made in fewer numbers. The old Sandwich dolphin candlesticks and Loop and Petal are rare, but religious crucifix candlesticks are often found and were not reproduced although they were late products. Syrup jugs and pitchers were made in many patterns. There were also interesting platters including bread platters impressed with "Give us this Day our Daily Bread" and a Liberty Bell platter. There were novelties including hand dishes, and bottles and vases in the shape of animals and national monuments. The small covered milk glass dishes are so popular with collectors today

Shaded opalescent ware, Beaumont Glass Co., Martins Ferry, Ohio—"Spanish Lace" types. LEFT TO RIGHT. Fluted bowl, fluted vase and syrup pitcher, clear with raised opalescent designs; cruet and large pitcher, cranberry with raised opalescence; Barber's Bottle, "Stars and Stripes" red with raised opalescence. (*The Chrysler Art Museum of Provincetown*)

Opaque glass. LEFT TO RIGHT. Candlesticks, fiery opalescent, Sandwich; pitcher, paneled Wheat Pattern, white, Hobbs, Brockunier & Co., Wheeling, W. Va.; stick vase, "Wheeling Peachblow," Hobbs, Brockunier; vase, blue opalene, Sandwich; box, white, "King Charles Spaniel," Sandwich; tumbler, Holly Amber, The Indiana Tumbler & Goblet Co., Greentown, Ind.; "Dolphin" covered dish, Chocolate glass; Holly Amber toothpick holder; "Rabbit" covered dish, Chocolate glass, Indiana Tumbler & Goblet Co. (*The Chrysler Art Museum of Provincetown*)

and are so characteristically Victorian that they require a chapter of their own.

Other types of opaque glass include Caramel Glass, Custard Glass, and rare Maize fashioned in little kernels to represent an ear of corn. This latter was made at the New England Glass Company in 1888. Marble Glass or Purple Slag is popular with collectors, but hard to find and therefore more expensive than other opaque glass. It was never made in such quantities as the opaque white glass and very few complete table settings were ever made. Such pieces as footed compotes, bowls, celery glasses, vases, and match holders and mugs are the articles to be found today.

In 1855 the New England Glass Company secured a patent for a curious Victorian novelty called silver glass. This glass had tremendous popularity in its day. It was first made as curtain pins, door knobs, and globes, but was later made in some tableware pieces such as goblets, wine glasses, salts, sugar bowls and pitchers as well as vases, candlesticks and paperweights. Some of this glass was plain, but other pieces were engraved or painted. Some of the silver glass vases were decorated in brilliant red, blue, and green and on others the designs were painted in opaque white. A few of the vases were gold, blue, or even lavender. Silver glass was made in two layers. The clear glass was first blown, later the nitrate of silver was blown into the hollow space between the layers through a hole in the base. Then the base was sealed. Nitrate of silver came in many colors.

Victorian vases were made in pairs. There are all types of vases from costly overlay to painted and enameled vases and those with applied decoration. There are both clear and opaque vases and those with a satin finish. There is no end of combinations of color. In shape and decoration these pairs of vases are perhaps the most characteristically Victorian of all Victorian glassware. Most of these vases are tall elongated shapes with scalloped and frilled tops or spreading flower lips. Some are made to sit on metal stands. Painted and enamel decoration includes birds and flowers in oriental style and groups of daisies and lilies of the valley. Others are decorated with Mary Gregory children. Colors range from lovely blues, pinks, and yellows of Satin Glass to the glossy tans and caramels and browns. Black glass vases with enameled flower decoration were especially popular. Another group had applied flowers or fruits. Silver glass vases were also made in pairs as were the various colors and sizes of satin glass rose bowls.

Louis C. Tiffany worked in stained glass for some years before he produced his first iridescent glass known as Favrile which was put on the market in 1896 and was made until about 1918. Tiffany glass reproduces the iridescence of ancient glass. Gold, amber, blue, and green were blended to produce a metallic iridescence. Although Tiffany drew on European and Oriental prototypes he also produced many striking and imaginative new forms. He was inspired by natural flower and plant forms—the peacock feather, and the growth and shells at the

bottom of the sea. Waves, clouds, and line effects that suggest the wind decorate some of the more imaginative pieces, but there were also more recognizable motifs such as vines, narcissus, lily of the valley, calla lily, and fish. The lily pad and mushroom were also favorite motifs.

Frederick Carder was another inspired glass designer. He developed Aurene glass in 1904. It has a smooth iridescent surface with ridges, grooves and crimped edges. The colors resemble those of the sunset, and the shapes are often twisted.

Quezal glass was made in imitation of Tiffany and Aurene. The leaf designs are usually green on a light gold ground. Vases and lampshades are the pieces available. Kew Blas made at Somerville, Massachusetts, is an iridescent glass with a smooth opalescent effect.

In about 1910, Carnival glass, an imitation of the finer iridescent glasswares, was made in great quantities to meet the popular demand. Carnival glass was a colored iridescent pressed glass. It was made by companies in Ohio, Pennsylvania and West Virginia, the most important of which were Imperial Glass Company and Northwood Glass Company. Carnival glass was made in a great variety of shapes, including pitchers and tumblers, goblets, cups, berry bowls and dishes, compotes, plates, sugar and creamers, vases, baskets, punch bowls, buttons, lamps and souvenirs. The colors range from shades of gold to red and from yellow green to deep blue or purple. A great many pieces of marigold, blue, purple, and amethyst were made, but comparatively few pieces of red, so that today red is the most expensive color. The patterns

Tiffany "Favrile" glass. TOP. Vases, leaf and full tulip designs. BOTTOM LEFT. Flared vase with peacock decoration. RIGHT. Leaf design vase. (*The Metropolitan Museum of Art*)

include fruit such as grapes and cherries, flowers, birds, butterflies and geometric designs.

Carnival glass is hardly an antique since it was made as late as the 1920's and is being reproduced in quantity today, but it is being collected and will certainly increase in price. However, it is not on the same plane as the other art glassware since it cannot claim artistic workmanship or good design. Nevertheless, like any other category, it can be fun collecting. (See illustration, page 155.)

Mrs. Rose M. Presznick sent me a copy of her *Carnival and Iridescent Glass Book III*. If I were a Carnival glass collector I would take her advice to "get on the old marigold, bronze, pastel, opalware and Imperial Jewels Art Glass wagon while it can be found at reasonable prices." I might add that from an artistic standpoint I consider these colorings the most attractive. Pieces of souvenir Carnival Glass are bound to increase in price because of their historic significance; also, if I were a button collector I would gather Carnival buttons while they can be found.

Iridescent glass. LEFT TO RIGHT. Blue & White, The Imperial Glass Co., Bellaire, Ohio; basket, gold, off-white & green, "Quezal," Quezal Art Glass & Decorating Co., Brooklyn, New York; vase, Jack-in-the-Pulpit style, gold, green and off-white, "Kew-Blas," Union Glass Co., Somerville, Mass.; finger bowl & saucer, gold and green with raised opalescent "jewels," "Aurene," Steuben Glass Works, Corning, N.Y.; fluted, footed vase, green with gold, Steuben. (*The Chrysler Art Museum of Provincetown*)

Silver vase. Designed by J. H. Whitehouse, Tiffany & Co. Presented to William Cullen Bryant, c. 1875. (*The Metropolitan Museum of Art*)

V. SILVER

Flatware

By 1840 silver was being made by machine, the day of the individual silversmith was ending, and silver companies were being established. However, contrary to common belief, fine silver was made in America throughout the nineteenth century. Spoons and other flatware continued to be made in a variation of the fiddle shape, but with an upturned spatulate handle. The thread design with a ridge outlining the handle was available in patterns called Plain Thread, French Thread, and Oval Thread. One with a shell at the end was a favorite. After 1860 the taste was for heavy ornate designs in high relief. The raised patterns were usually stamped or cast and designs were of various types including naturalistic flowers, conventional, and geometric. In 1871 Tiffany brought out the Japanese pattern in flat silver. It was a design with naturalistic birds, flowers and grasses, and no two pieces were alike. This design reflects the great interest in Japanese art. It is now being made again from the old dies.

The influence of Greek mythology was dominant in the Olympian group of flatware which Tiffany exhibited in Paris in 1878. A description of these pieces will give a good idea of the designs and the elaborateness of the silverware made in America at this date. These

187

descriptions are condensed from the Tiffany folder in the Landauer Collection at the New-York Historical Society.

SOUP LADLE—Jupiter with eagle and sceptre surrounded by gods and goddesses on Mt. Olympus. On the back is Cupid with torch and bow.

OYSTER LADLE—Hebe, cupbearer of gods is watched over by the eagle of Jove. On the back, wine vessel, barley and horn of plenty. On heel, head of Jupiter crowned with olive wreath.

BERRY AND SALAD SPOONS—Paris presenting golden apple to Venus.

TABLESPOON—Venus in shell drawn by dolphins driven by Cupid. On back, emblems of love—myrtle, doves, torches and burning heart.

DESSERT SPOON—Orpheus in search of Eurydice; on back, male and female heads with lyre and laurel.

TEASPOON—Diana and nymphs surprised by Pan. On back, dead stag.

COFFEE SPOON—Bacchantes and infant Bacchus. On back, head of faun, doves.

TABLE FORK. Hercules and Omphale.

DESSERT FORK—Sybil unrolling scrolls of fate.

MEAT CARVER—4th Labor of Hercules.

GAME CARVER—Actaeon devoured by dogs. On back, stag's head and implements of hunting.

DINNER KNIFE—Bacchus feeding the sacred panther.

BREAKFAST KNIFE—Orpheus charming wild animals.

DESSERT KNIFE—Bacchus and Bacchante.

NUT PICKS—2nd labor of Hercules.

MUSTARD SPOON—Sleeping Diana.

SALT SPOON—Satyrs and Sylvanus.

The designs were stamped on these pieces and the work was finished by hand. Gorham also made a heavy ornate pattern called "Raphael," and "King" and "Hindostanee" were the new patterns brought out by them in 1878. In the 1880's and 1890's the designs of American silverware were varied and selected from many sources.

There was a revival of the elaborate old French forms and borrowing from the Orient and the Near East. Gorham put out the "Medici" and "Fontainebleau" patterns in 1882 and the Sheaf of Wheat in 1887. However, these are expensive exhibition pieces and were probably only made to special order. The most of the flat silver available for the average American table in the 1890's was much simpler. It included fine-cut engraved patterns in such designs as "Lily," "Daisy," "Clover," "Wheat," "Windsor" and "Clifton." Other patterns such as "Antique" made by Whiting & Co. of New York had an allover chased pattern with a small panel left for a monogram. Such plain patterns as "Oval Thread," "Plain Thread," "French Thread" and "Plain Tip" continued to be made. Many decorative patterns were made only in teaspoons. Such patterns as "Egyptian," "Persian," "Tuscan," "Athenian" and "Alhambra" reflect the decorative interest of the times. A pattern called "Ivy" had a design of strapwork and a mask which relates it to the Renaissance Revival. Whiting & Co. made a die-pressed spoon in

Silver patterns made by Whiting & Co. in the 1870's, still popular in the 1890's. LEFT TO RIGHT. Oval Thread, Plain Thread, Persian, Plain Tip, Japanese (bamboo), Honeysuckle. (*Jewelers' Circular Keystone*)

Japanese pattern similar to the Japanese design made by Tiffany. The "Honeysuckle" was a related pattern which was made by Whiting & Co. Whiting also made a grape pattern which is Victorian in spirit, and Theodore Starr made a very attractive die-stamped chrysanthemum pattern.

In the 1890's the craze for souvenir spoons promoted the sale of silver and it became fashionable to assemble sets of tea or coffee spoons as souvenirs of different cities and states. These spoons were made of sterling silver and many of the designs are attractive, but their real value is historic since they preserve landmarks no longer in existence such as the old Cliff House in San Francisco and Castle Garden, New York. Souvenir spoon collecting is an interesting and inexpensive hobby related to the American Victorian period.

Almost all of the flat silver patterns are available to collectors today. However, it may take years to assemble a complete set, but many of the patterns such as Tiffany's "Japanese" ("Audubon") and Whiting's "Japanese" ("Bamboo") and "Honeysuckle" are similar and

Group of nineteenth century spoons that reflect the popular design motifs of the era. LEFT TO RIGHT. Ivy, Grape, Egyptian, Alhambra, Italian. (*Jewelers' Circular Keystone*)

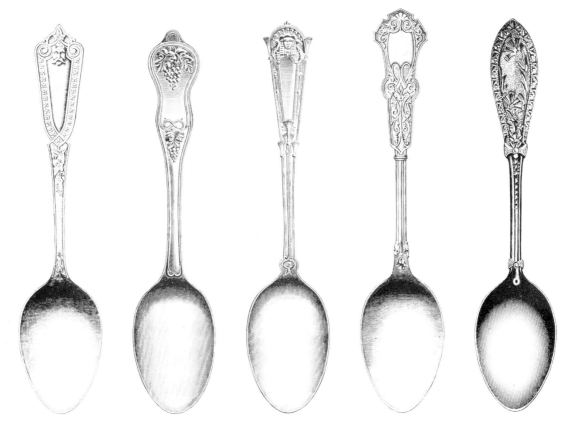

Tiffany Japanese pattern 1871, now called Audubon (*Tiffany & Co.*)

could be used together. There are also many patterns such as "Old King" and "Imperial Queen" which have a shell or anthemion motif which harmonize with each other. When buying old nineteenth century American silver one must remember that the patterns were made in several weights and the heaviness will determine the price as will the scarcity and demand.

In the 1860's the word sterling came into use and silver was marked "Sterling." Also patterns were patented at about this same time and the patent date of the pattern indicates when it was first made. For example, Tiffany's Olympian is marked "Tiffany Sterling Pat. 1878" although it is still being made. Since all of this late American silver is marked it is easy to identify and one can be sure of what one owns. While the prices of these old flat silver pieces are no longer cheap, they are less than the new pieces of the same pattern and a set could thus be assembled with part old and part new pieces at less expense.

Hollow Ware

THE hollow ware reflects the decorative styles of the Victorian period more closely than the flatware. Shapes of Victorian hollow ware changed along with styles and design motifs of the furniture of the period. The characteristics of the Empire style persisted in the silver of the 1840's as they did in furniture and decorative accessories. As the period opens

Silver tea set. Ball, Tompkins & Black, New York, c. 1845. (*The Henry Ford Museum*)

Sterling silver tea and coffee service. Samuel Kirk 1824. This style continued through 1840's.

the classical Empire style with fluted body and pedestal base is characteristic of the tea and coffee service. The gadroon, Greek key, laurel or acanthus decoration was heavy and embossed and shows the influence of the rococo revival. There was also some Etruscan influence and decorative processes included chasing, engraving and pierced work. Some of the companies working in New York at this date were: J. H. Johnston; Wood & Hughes; Ball, Tompkins & Black, and William Gale & Son; in Philadelphia, R. & W. Wilson; Bailey & Kitchen. The bodies of their tea sets were ovoid with incurvate necks and the repoussé decoration abounded in "C" scrolls and moulded grapes. Garlands of oak and acorns, and rustic twig handles and flower finials gave an appearance of abundance.

Samuel Kirk of Baltimore had introduced repoussé decoration as early as 1824 and by the middle of the century the rococo influence was seen in the allover naturalistic repoussé patterns made not only by Samuel Kirk & Son of Baltimore, but by Tiffany & Co. of New York and Gorham Co. of Providence, R.I. The forms of the pieces became wider, deeper, and exaggerated. The bodies were pear-shaped or spherical and handles were covered with leaf ornament. The spout of the teapot and coffee pot often ended in a bird's beak. Grape vines entwined rustic branches on handles, and finials were birds, deer, flowers, or pineapple forms. An ad of 1853 showed a tea set covered with a raised grape pattern and a centerpiece of an oak tree with branches holding glass bowls for fruit. At the base were figures of deer standing on a ground of grasses and fallen leaves. Hexagonal-shaped low-slung forms were covered with engraved patterns of rococo cartouches which sometimes enclosed scenes. In New York Tiffany & Co. sold silver made by Gorham & Co. and Ball, Black & Co. was also a fashionable store. In Philadelphia, P. L. Krider, J. E. Caldwell & Co. and Bailey & Co. were the principal companies.

In the 1860's–70's Elizabethan Renaissance hollow ware shapes were low-slung ovals, or angular with borders of conventional ivy, acanthus, strapwork and other architectural details. The Greek "oenoche" form with hoof-feet was seen in coffee pots. Gradually there was an increased

Silver tea set. William F. Ladd, New York, c. 1850. (*The New-York Historical Society*)

exaggeration of form and elaboration of design. Feet made up of exaggerated scrolls of acanthus leaves took the place of bases. Dulled and matted finishes gave a contrast of texture and an illusion of realism. By the 1870's the machine age produced designs that were a mass of over-elaborate rich decoration. An author writing in 1870 speaks of the after-dinner coffee pot with a long and slender neck made of hand-hammered silver by Kirk, and a coffee pot of niello-work made by Tiffany. Some silver services were made with no two pieces alike. A coffee pot with acorn and oak leaves had a modified Persian shape, and a Grecian-shaped vase with openwork handles made by Gorham had plaques of Thorwaldsen's "Night" and "Morning" with draperies of gold and oxide tints. Aurora and Venus motifs were seen in an elaborate centerpiece. Also, the naturalistic Japanese influence remained popular and etching and niello added richness.

Centerpieces for fruit and flowers were in great demand. These pieces allowed the designer to use his imagination and ingenuity both in the design and workmanship. There were centerpieces of Greek chariots drawn by cupids. These were ornamented with bas reliefs and burnished, and the edges and rims were touched with gold. A silver fruit service designed by Gorham consisted of a tall bowl set on a tripod of Egyptian design fastened to a heavy base. Two smaller matching bowls complete the centerpiece. Another elaborate flower and fruit piece consisted of four matching vases supported by female figures. It was set on a plateau of glass.

A writer in the *Art Journal,* 1875, says: "It was thought that the introduction of electro-plated ware would lessen the demand for solid silver objects but this is not so. The production of the artistic designs of the Meriden Company and other electro-plating corporations appears to have stimulated the taste for the beautiful and our manufactures of solid silverware are not only the equal in gracefulness and originality in the ateliers of England and France, but they are annually rapidly approximating it in value and volume." He mentions Tiffany, Gorham, and Whiting & Co. of New York City and goes on to state: "Machinery is not used to any considerable extent in the manufacture of silver-work if we except certain specialties, such as spoons and forks; and even of

Silver fruit dish. Tiffany & Co. (*The Art Journal*, 1876)

these many are still made by hand though the ornaments on the handle are generally produced by stamping or by letting the object pass between rollers or discs on which the pattern is cut. But in the production of silver design of a high character, machinery performs only a small part.''

Through the influence of the Centennial in 1876 and the large plated and silver pieces displayed by such companies as Tiffany, Gorham, Reed and Barton, and Meriden Britannia, the historical and genre influence seen in the painting of the period was reflected in the design of silverware which became literary and story-telling. On the Century Vase exhibited by Gorham we see the story of the progress of American manufactures. There are scenes of pioneer days, Indians, fruits, flowers, and agrarian motifs such as wheat, scythe, plow and beehives which relate to the American scene. Another piece which showed American originality in design motifs was the Bryant Testimonial Vase made by Tiffany. The vase is covered with a meshwork of apple branches, primrose, amaranth and other flowers mentioned in Bryant's poems. The vase is monumental and symbolical in conception, but the design motifs are for the most part original and represent American ideas.

Although American silver designers continued to create new designs, the impact of mechanization had stamped out the craft of the silversmith and his work was mostly taken over by factory processes. Such was the elaborateness of the styles and the demand for large presentation and testimonial pieces, loving cups and trophies, that the large companies such as Gorham, Tiffany, Whiting & Co., Starr & Marcus, and Black Starr & Frost, found it necessary to employ artistic designers and craftsmen to supply their trade. James H. Whitehouse was the top designer at Tiffany. Gorham's head designers were T. J. Pairpont and William Codman, and Charles Osborne was employed by Whiting & Co. These designers worked on the production of testimonials, racing trophies and presentation pieces that were the major products of the silver companies of the late nineteenth century. Extreme style and decorative abandon resulted in flamboyant designs which were a combination of

Silver centerpiece. Gorham Manufacturing Co. (*The Art Journal,* 1876)

naturalistic decoration and heroic subjects from Greek mythology. The popular shapes were vases, bowls and urns. In addition to repoussé and cast reliefs the pieces were chased and engraved, and techniques of matting, frosting, burnishing, oxidation and parcel gilt enriched the surfaces.

The silver which Tiffany exhibited in Paris in 1900 was completely eclectic. There were vases and bowls with ears of corn and jewels in Aztec style, a Zuni Indian basket-shaped bowl, and a bowl in the shape of a Hupa Indian basket with rattlesnake handles. A loving cup illustrated the Indian war dance and had buffalo horn handles. Another was a Sitka Indian design and had Rocky Mountain sheep horns for handles. One coffee pot was in Byzantine style, and another Egyptian. A silver service of 110 pieces in George III style had modeled figures and pierced and chased designs, while a tea set was embossed with a design of American flowers including poppies, buttercups, apple blossoms, dogwood and lily of the valley.

There is not a great deal of American Victorian silver on the market today because there has been so little demand for it that it has not come out of attic hiding. Now and again such pieces come up at auction and there are pieces to be seen in some museums and historical societies. For the most part these pieces were given to the museums, but within the last few years museums have actually been collecting nineteenth century American silver, for example, the Metropolitan Museum of Art to add to the collection of its American Wing. This silver is all marked and the marks are recorded so that there is no difficulty in identifying the maker. There is practically no literature on the subject.

Presentation Silver and Silver Plate

PRESENTATION silver is primarily of historic interest although many pieces are of artistic value and are the work of prominent American silversmiths.

Silversmiths were engaged in making presentation silver almost from the beginning of American history. The first pieces made were given to churches and are to be seen today in such collections as that of Trinity

Church, New York City. Silver presentation pieces were also awarded to college tutors and military men, and there were medals and gorgets given to peace-loving Indians. The most of these pieces are early and they are in museums and historical societies. But there are nineteenth century presentation pieces which have found their way to pawn shops and to second-hand silver shops, and are thus available to collectors to-day. There were pieces which were given as awards to encourage agriculture and business, as well as historical presentation pieces. There were sports trophies for yachting and racing, and cups for best-of-breed dogs and other animals. It is in this field of lesser presentation pieces that the collector will find articles for his collection.

These pieces are interesting because they reflect the shapes and motifs of the American Victorian era. Many show unique and indigenous designs. There are silver vases which have sculptured motifs of American produce such as the Heinz Trophy which was awarded to the district that sold the most Heinz products. The superintendent of the district that won the award for three years was allowed to keep the cup. This vase, with a sculptured group of tomatoes, cucumbers and other vegetables,

Silver Salver showing Brick Church, New York. Made by Ball, Black & Co., 1860. (*The New-York Historical Society*)

should be extant today, and if the owner should need money might come on the market. Many nineteenth century yachting trophies, although made of fine silver, are not always artistic in design, and when the yacht club is no longer in existence they are often disposed of. Then there are the plated trophies and prize cups which have little artistic or intrinsic value but which give a picture of other days and record a forgotten event. There is the plated silver tea set with the inscription, "Given to Mr. and Mrs. Amberson McClinton by the Pastime Social Club," which pictures a way of life no longer in existence.

All of these articles represent the minor side of presentation silver collecting but articles which represent major collecting interests are also available. There are trays and vases with engraved scenes of buildings and ships no longer in existence. One interesting tray has vignette scenes of San Francisco, including Seal Rocks and the old Cliff House. There are also pieces displaying historical sites with appropriate inscriptions and dates.

LEFT. Silver tea kettle made by Wm. Gale & Son. Presented to Commodore Matthew Calbraith Perry, 1855. RIGHT. Silver tea kettle showing Egyptian influence. Tiffany & Co. Presented to yacht "Mallory," 1862. (*The New-York Historical Society*)

Silver trinket box. Gorham Manufacturing Co., c. 1880. Presented to Emma C. Thursby by Gilmore's Band. (*The New-York Historical Society*)

Presentation swords are a major field for collectors. In recent years sword collecting has become a popular hobby in America and the collecting of presentation swords is a specialized category. Washington's swords on display at Mount Vernon were made by European swordsmiths. But American silversmiths were making dress-sword hilts as early as 1770; Paul Revere's books reveal that he made silver sword hilts. There are early sword hilts with lion, dog and eagle-head pommels made by such silversmiths as Jacob Hurd of Boston and William Moulton. Isaac Hutton of Albany, who worked as late as 1855, made stylized eagle-head hilts. The majority of the early presentation swords are in museums and historical societies but some are in private collections. There are presentation swords of the War of 1812, the Mexican War, the Civil War, and the Spanish-American War, as well as World War I, which are available for collectors today.

As time went on the trend toward ornateness in sword hilts increased. Some hilts had a plumed and helmeted head as a pommel motif. The presentation sword of the Civil War was a popular and representative piece of Victorian goldsmith's work. These hilts reflected the ornate

baroque taste of the times. The swords were massive and heavily ornamented, with sculptured mountings of rich metals and precious stones.
The grips had figures of soldiers, sailors, the Goddess of Liberty, classical figures and patriotic insignia. The hilts were made by such well-
known silver companies as Tiffany, Gorham, and Samuel Kirk & Son.
In 1862 Tiffany made presentation swords which were given to the Civil
War heroes, Major General Halleck, Major General Fremont and
Major General Burnside. These were presented by states, cities and
patriotic organizations. After the Civil War officers' swords were simpler,
and the practice of presenting dress swords went out of style after World
War I.

Another piece of presentation silver available to the collector today

LEFT. Hilt of sword presented to Gen. William T. Sherman. Pommel decorated with stars and
mounted with eagle. Goddess Athena in grip niche. RIGHT. Hilt of sword presented to Major
General Winfield Scott Hancock. Ornamented with patriotic symbols. c. 1861. (*Smithsonian
Institution*)

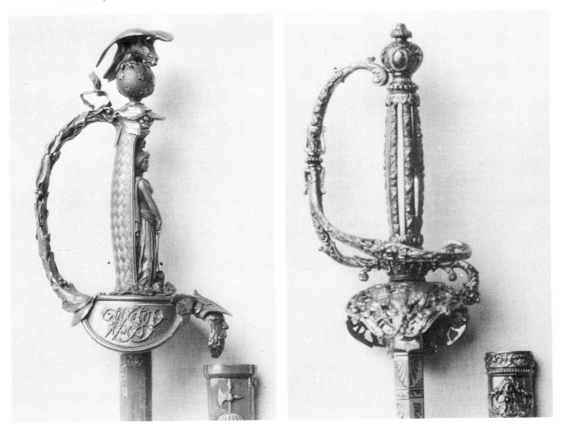

is the silver trumpet. Silver trumpets were the popular trophies given to persons for their heroism at fires or for their work in volunteer fire companies.

The volunteer fire department was an important factor in the political and social life of the American city for several centuries, and it continued to function until the end of the nineteenth century. Today the old fire engines and many of the articles used in early fire fighting, such as hats, leather buckets, signal torches and lanterns, are collector's items. One of the most interesting objects was the fire trumpet. The brass speaking trumpet was used by the foreman of the volunteer fire department to shout directions and to encourage the men fighting the fire. Nineteenth century prints of fires and firemen, such as those by T. W. Strong and Currier and Ives, show the foreman with his trumpet.

In the late nineteenth century it became the custom to present a silver trumpet for heroism at fires and as a recognition of honor for work in a volunteer fire department. These trumpets were ornamented with the symbol of the fire company. The symbols included such motifs as the Beehive, the Eagle, Tiger, Neptune, and other appropriate devices. The trumpets were also engraved with elaborate scroll decoration which might include a picture of the engine, and an inscription which included the name, date, and particular incident of bravery for which the trumpet was presented. They were also hung with bright silk cords. Many of these silver presentation trumpets, including the one belonging to Boss Tweed of New York, are in present-day collections and some are still available for the collector.

Still another presentation piece was the silver trowel. The use of a silver trowel to lay the cornerstone of a public building was a late nineteenth century custom. These trowels were inscribed with the occasion, date and names of the person who laid the stone, the building committee and the architect. A collection of these presentation trowels would not only tell the story of many well-known buildings, but would also include the names of late nineteenth century silversmiths and silver companies.

TOP. Silver Presentation Trumpet, c. 1880's. (*The H. V. Smith Museum of the Home Insurance Co.*)
BOTTOM. Silver trowel. Gorham & Co., 1914. (*The New-York Historical Society*)

There are also yachting trophies and other sports trophies, including baseball, tennis, bicycle racing, horse racing and golf. Many of these are in club collections but others are owned by the individuals who won them. They are often found in pawn shops and second-hand silver shops. The yachting trophies are not only unique in design, with motifs relating to the sea and racing, but they often preserve the pictures of famous boats and give their names, the dates of the races and the names of the persons who presented the trophies. Silver trophies have some artistic and intrinsic value. The plated trophies have value as a picture of popular art of another century. Those including models of old bicycles or golfing figures in knickers and other outdated paraphernalia are amusing as well as possessing a certain historical significance. They also give a picture of the bad taste of much of the silver and plated ware of the late nineteenth century.

One of the most interesting and little known fields of American silversmiths' work was the production of presentation silver for battleships and cruisers of the United States Navy. These were made in the 1890's and they represent the finest design and workmanship of the American silversmith of the late nineteenth century. They are not available for collections.

The most important presentation piece of the Victorian era was the Bryant Testimonial Vase, which was given to the poet William Cullen Bryant and is now in the Metropolitan Museum, New York City. This piece is described here because it gives an excellent picture of American nineteenth century silversmiths' work.

Silver salver with scenes of San Francisco including the Cliff House and Presidio. Made by Vanderslice & Co., and presented to John S. Ellis in 1864. (*The New-York Historical Society*)

As we see the vase today it is covered with a fretwork of apple blossoms and branches designed to express the bloom and wholesome freshness of Bryant's poetry. Beneath the fretwork are primrose and amaranth, and gentian which refers to the poem, "Fringed Gentian." The poems "Water Fowl", "Robert of Lincoln", "The Planting of the Apple Tree", "Forest Hymn" and "Thanatopsis" are all suggested in the design, which includes a beautiful border of Indian corn, water lilies and handles that enclose the bobolink. There are medallions of the poet's bust and scenes from Bryant's life. The vase is typical of the literary silver pieces of the late nineteenth century. The design inspired by a combination of classic and Japanese influence is nevertheless distinctly American in its use of indigenous plants, flowers and subject matter. It was designed by James Whitehouse of Tiffany & Co. The piece cost $5000, but copies were available at $500.

Electroplate

ELECTROPLATE is one of the most characteristic products of the Victorian era. This pseudo-silver provided ostentation and dining table elegance at small cost and immediately captured the popular fancy. Any article, no matter how elaborate, that could be made in silver could be reproduced in electroplate for half the price. Electroplate is made by electrolysis. In a bath of potassium cyanide, silver is decomposed and deposited on a base metal surface such as copper, britannia, white metal, or later, German nickel. John O. Mead of Philadelphia was the earliest electroplater in America. His business, first listed in 1840, never rivalled the larger companies and no pieces have been found with his marks, although in 1859 he had a thriving commercial trade. The companies who are best known in the early electroplate field in America were Reed and Barton, Meriden Britannia, and Rogers Brothers. In the post-Civil War period there were many other important companies making electroplate such as Oneida, Gorham, and Rice.

Electroplate sports trophies. (*Reed & Barton Catalogue, 1885*)

Electroplate centerpiece, The Barge of Venus. Middletown Silverplate Company. (*The Art Journal,* 1875)

America got its first look at electroplate at the Centennial in 1876. The large companies who were makers of electroplate displayed ornate exhibition pieces. Meriden Britannia exhibited a large Neptune epergne with hanging dishes for fruit and bonbons. At the base were figures of Neptune and Earth. They also exhibited a group of figures called Buffalo Hunt. Reed and Barton exhibited their Progress Vase surmounted by the figure of Liberty, which stood on a base with sculptured groups of the landing of Columbus and a group of primitive Aztec Indians on horseback. Middletown Silver Plate Co. exhibited an elaborate plateau centerpiece on which the shell-shaped barge of Venus was drawn by two swans driven by Cupid. Such pieces as these attracted wide attention and created a demand for plated ware. Hotels were soon supplied with huge coffee urns and tea services; every housewife owned an electroplated tea set, and a centerpiece and casters were on every dining table.

Catalogues illustrating electroplate were brought out by the principal companies in the 1860's, 1870's, and 1880's, and these give an idea of the extent of the articles available in electroplate. Tableware was made in the greatest quantities. Pieces included tureens, waiters, vegetable and pudding dishes, candelabra, wine coolers, casters, bread trays, butter dishes, pitchers, fruit stands, berry bowls, cake baskets and tea and coffee sets. The most popular item was the tea set which was usually included among every middle-class bride's wedding gifts. It consisted of from five to seven pieces although early sets before 1850 were usually made in only three pieces. While the designs of tea sets varied from decade to decade, the sets made by the different companies at the same date had little variation in their basic shapes.

The shapes and designs of plated ware are closely related to silver shapes of the same period. The early sets made in the 1850's are large

Silver-plate tea and coffee service. Webster Mfg. Co., Brooklyn, 1859–1873. (*The International Silver Company*)

Floral embossed tea set. Meriden Britannia Co. 1886. (*The International Silver Co.*)

Silver-plated water pitcher on stand with goblet. Meriden Britannia Co., Patented 1868. (*The Henry Ford Museum*)

and stand on high pedestal bases. The decoration varies from plain panels to ornate grape patterns, and handles are often made of wood. The urn shape on a pedestal continued into the 1860's, but the handles are of curved metal. The finials in the shape of fruits, birds or flowers are attached with a screw. Instead of embossing, the patterns are formed by chasing, or cutting. Borders are foliated, beaded or gadroon. The chief manufacturers of this period were Meriden Britannia, Reed and Barton, Rogers, and Gorham.

By 1870 the teapot and other pieces are set on legs instead of on a pedestal and the handles are angular. Deep-chased patterns include exotic birds and Egyptian motifs with raised applied bands. In the 1880's the shape changes to a low, broad form set on a rim base instead of legs. The surface was ornamented with ferns, flowers and grasses in bright-cut designs upon a "frosted" background. Later embossed and repoussé allover and hammered designs were popular, and the teapot and coffee pot were smaller in size. Hotel ware was simple in form and decorated with plain fluted or gadroon borders on a pearl-finish body. Trays and hot water kettles usually matched the tea sets.

Ice water pitchers, especially the tilting pitcher, which was set on a tray with matching goblets, is another Victorian electroplate article

Silver-plated tea service. Renaissance Revival, c. 1875. (*The Henry Ford Museum*)

which is collected today. The ice water pitcher dates from a patent of 1854 acquired by the Meriden Britannia Company, but it was also made by several other companies. The earliest ice water pitchers were of simple design, held from two to four quarts and sat on a tray with one goblet. Later the pitchers became larger and more ornate, sometimes decorated with a snow scene. Many pitchers were mounted on tilting racks, with two goblets. In 1886 Meriden Britannia offered 57 different designs of ice water pitchers. By the 1890's the water pitcher is smaller and is usually set on a matching tray with a set of goblets. Elaborate covered punch bowls set on a tray or plateau with a set of twelve "glasses" were probably made as presentation pieces or for special groups. These are rare and were expensive when made and are seldom on the market today. Covered tureens, vegetable dishes, and other serving dishes were made in quantity.

The revolving caster was one of the most widely used pieces of electroplate. According to directions for setting the table given in cookbooks of the period, the caster should sit in the center of the table. Casters had been used on the table early in the nineteenth century, but the early type of casters set on a footed tray with center handle were

Silver-plated casters. Meriden Britannia Company, 1870's. (*The International Silver Company*)

not made in electroplate. The earliest electroplate caster has a wide pierced band which serves as a holder for the bottles. There are usually six bottles and sometimes small salt dips. The base is set on four feet and the bottom is often wood. An ornate handle is in the center. Casters of 1860 are more elaborate and the bottles are of pressed glass patterns. Pressed glass caster bottles were made in the following patterns: Bellflower, Daisy & Button, Beaded Dewdrop, Beaded Grape, Medallion Bull's Eye, Fine Cut, Fine Rib, Gothic, Hamilton, Ivy, Honeycomb, Palmette, Powder & Shot, Thumbprint, Roman Rosette and Eugenia. Caster bottles were also made in many cut glass patterns. The rotary caster was patented in 1862. The bottles fitted into holes on a circular platform which stood on a tall cone-type base and the center handle was often decorated with elaborate openwork design. In the 1870's heavy grape and beaded borders were added. Later, the low caster came back into vogue and colored pressed glass containers with Daisy and Button pattern or milk opalescent or cased glass were popular and the silver frame was reduced to a few wires. There were also pickle and salad casters. The most interesting feature of these late casters was the container. In addition to pressed glass of blue, canary or crystal, they were made of Pomona art glass, opalene twist, imported, decorated ruby glass and cut crystal. The glass containers had a fancy plated cover and decorated tongs were fastened to the stand.

Silver-plated pickle casters. TOP RIGHT. Container Pomona Glass. Meriden Britannia Company, 1870's. (*The International Silver Company*)

Silver centerpiece, "Hiawatha's Canoe." Gorham Manufacturing Company. (*The Art Journal*, 1875)

Trays of all sizes—oval, round, and rectangular—were made with gadroon or fluted borders in plain or satin finish. They were also made with repoussé borders and fancy corners, including Egyptian heads. Etched or chased designs of flowers, birds, and grasses as well as scenes decorated the centers of some trays. Cake baskets with handles stood on legs or center standards.

The most interesting and also one of the expensive electroplated items is the Victorian fruit, berry dish, or centerpiece. This piece is of special interest to collectors because of the glass dish which is set in the frame. Many of these dishes have been taken out of the electroplate framework and sold separately, but now the collector is searching for the complete piece. This, when found, is expensive. The catalogue price was about a tenth of the present asking price. However, many of the stands with their ruffled bowls of various types of American and European Victorian glassware are decorative. Practically every American glass manufacturer made glass containers for these electroplate stands. Pressed glass from the various Pittsburgh factories and clear, colored, and Mary Gregory glass from Sandwich and New England Glass Company were the most common varieties. But there were also containers of hob nail, Satin glass, Wheeling Peachblow, Pomona, Amberina and Burmese glass. Some of the finest pieces have containers of frosted glass with etched designs and some had cut-glass bowls. Parker and Casper & Co. of W. Meriden, Connecticut, in an ad of 1869, stated: "Cutting of glassware used by us in caster, wine, and pickle frames, berry dishes, gives an advantage over other manufacturers." Bohemian, Venetian, Bristol, and Nailsea glass containers were also used.

LEFT. Fruit dish with figure of Cupid, herringbone Satin glass bowl on silver-plated stand by Wilcox Silver Plate Co. CENTER. Plated stand with bowl of pink Satin glass. RIGHT. Bowl, Amberina glass, New England Glass Co. (*The Corning Museum of Glass*)

The centerpiece usually consisted of a tall fruit dish on a metal stand with two lower matching dishes. There were also centerpieces set on a glass plateau. One by Reed and Barton consists of a peacock drawing a chariot which holds a glass container for flowers. Another centerpiece is a rowboat holding children, while Meriden Britannia made a delicate sailboat set on a plateau. A bowl for fruit is set on a pedestal from which springs a decorative vine-entwined arm holding a cornucopia-shaped glass vase for flowers. These were illustrated in advertisements of 1879. Gorham's fruit and flower services had Grecian figures, festoons, and gilded bas reliefs. Many small tablewares such as spoon racks on stands, syrup pitchers, butter dishes, toothpick holders, knife rests, bells, napkin rings and children's mugs are available for the collector with a small purse. Such articles as napkin rings, toothpick holders or children's mugs can form an amusing collection and these small items

LEFT. Satin glass, herringbone design bowl, plated stand, Derby Silver Co., c. 1885. CENTER. Bowl, Peachblow, New England Glass Co.; stand, Simpson, Hall, Miller & Co. RIGHT. Bowl, Satin glass with enamel decoration; stand, Meriden Britannia Co. (*Corning Museum of Glass*)

Silver-plated epergne. Simpson, Hall, Miller Co. Bowls decorated Burmese glass. Mt. Washington Glass Co. (*The Corning Museum of Glass*)

probably tell us more about late Victorian electroplate than almost any other articles.

The popularity of electroplate lasted until late in the century. The falling price of silver then made it possible for those who wanted silver to buy sterling. Although electroplate was first developed in England, American electroplate is superior to the English product, but great quantities of both were made and are available for collectors today. Electroplate is usually marked. Before 1860 the marks were on discs soldered to the bottom of the piece, afterwards the marks were cut directly into the bottom of the piece. The mark included the maker's name and trademark and often the word "triple," "quadruple," or "quadruple plate." Any numbers under the name refer to the pattern. From year to year maker's marks often vary. Electroplate was made in sets and it is not difficult to assemble matching pieces of a tea set or goblets to match a tipping-pitcher. Early electroplate is hard to find and of course more valuable. Some of the early pieces are not marked with the maker's name. The base metal on which the silver is plated partly determines the value. Gorham always produced high class electroplate and together with Reed and Barton used a heavy nickel silver base where many other companies used a lightweight white metal or Britannia. Meriden also used a Britannia base in the 1870's.

The condition of a piece of electroplate is not as important as it might seem, since no matter how battered or worn the scars and scratches can be repaired and the piece can be replated. Since electroplate can be dipped and polished with little time and effort, the collector would first of all do well to buy pieces by well-known makers such as Gorham or Reed and Barton, and also have a reputable shop do the repair job. Gorham is the highest grade electroplate, and is indistinguishable from pure silver in both style and appearance. Since Gorham made electroplate for only a few years, pieces of their plate are not plentiful.

Small Plated Tablewares

In the search to find inexpensive American Victorian antiques for the collector, small articles of electroplate stand out as a comparatively unexplored field. Small objects were made for the desk, such as inkwells; there were match safes for the gentlemen and chatelaine purses, vinaigrette and hairpin holders for the ladies, but the small accessories for use on the dining table are especially interesting and available. There are numerous small articles such as napkin rings, knife rests, mugs, goblets, toothpick holders, trays and small candlesticks which have been neglected by collectors. These things were all made from the 1870's to the end of the century.

Napkin rings are the most interesting category because of their various forms and the unique, typically Victorian designs. The first patent for napkin rings was taken out in 1869 although they were illustrated in catalogues a few years earlier. There are plain napkin rings with chased initials, names, or floral designs in satin finish; scroll embossed patterns, and rings decorated with hammering. Some rings had contrasting shiny beaded, fluted or plain borders and some had borders of open work. The subject matter of many of these designs on napkin rings is fascinating. Sculptured fruit such as cherries and gooseberries, flowers including lilies and roses, a snail and shell, a frog and lily pad, a dog house with a dog at the door, butterflies and fans, are only a few of the Victorian fancies available to the collector of napkin rings.

However, the figure designs are the most interesting. These have standing figures of people, usually cupids or boys and girls. There are quaint children in Kate Greenaway costume—a little girl is dressed in coat, bonnet and muff, and a boy is in coveralls with a frilled collar. Other children are shown with pets or playing games, such as the children climbing a ladder. There were many napkin rings with animals, and birds. The goat was a favorite, as were the rabbit, squirrel, dog and kitten. There were also hens, roosters, birds, ducks and a cow and

Group of silver-plated napkin rings. (*The International Silver Company*)

camel. The figure usually stands beside the ring and is soldered to it, but some are set on platforms. A combination of a figure of a cupid or butterfly holding a small vase for flowers is rare and thus expensive. Figures of dogs, goats, ponies, or children drawing a two-wheeled cart on which the napkin ring is placed are also rare. A clumsy combination of salt, pepper, butter plate and napkin ring set on a stand with a handle is also hard to find.

In addition to rarity of subject matter the collector should look for the markings. Besides the maker's name or trade mark, the piece was often marked "Triple" or "Quadruple" plate which gives a clue as to quality.

Plated knife rests are also amusing to collect. There are rests upheld by squirrels, chicks, dogs and other animals. The same animals and Victorian children hold barrel toothpick holders set on a stand. A porcupine with holes for the toothpicks is rare.

In the Reed & Barton catalogue of 1885, trays, or waiters as they were called, were made with chased designs in various types of finishes —pearl finish, Persian finish, and Oriental. The designs for the most part are of Oriental inspiration including birds, butterflies or dragonflies, and sprays of bamboo and oriental blossoms. Other designs include groups of naturalistic spring flowers or a spray of geraniums, while still other trays have scenes with cupids or draped figures. There are trays with center designs of a chased dog or cat head with a raised

Silver-plated trays. (*Reed & Barton Catalogue 1885*)

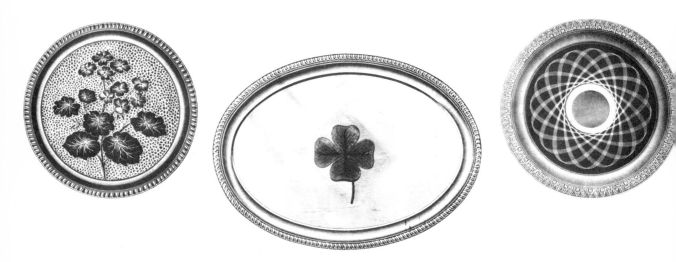

border of birds and flowers. A plain waiter has a geometric pattern or a four-leaf clover in its center, and there are hotel waiters in all sizes with plain, fluted or gadroon edges. Small card plates had similar designs. The crumb tray and scraper was etched with a floral design or a romantic scene of figures and wooded scenery.

Plated candlesticks of the various pedestal types were made in pairs. There were also saucer types, and later four- and five-branch candelabra were made. While there were plain sticks with round and square bases decorated with fluting and beaded bands, the fanciful decorated type seems to have been more popular. In Reed & Barton's catalogue of 1884, in addition to pedestal candlesticks with and without etched wind glasses, there are many small low candlesticks with griffin handles. These were variations of the saucer type and include a grape design socket set on a leaf saucer, a socket with lily pad saucer, and a socket set on a resting camel's back. A candlestick for the horseman includes a horse's head, stirrup and strap. A Victorian pedestal vase also held a candle socket. These candlesticks are marked with the maker's name. The ones marked "Rogers 1847" were made after 1900. The plain candlesticks and candelabra are in demand as substitutes for more expensive Sheffield Plate, but the fancy types when found should be less expensive and amusing to own.

Silver-plated candlesticks. (*Reed & Barton Catalogue 1885*)

Shell and Seaweed patterns of majolica from the collection of Mr. and Mrs. Ellis E. Stern.

VI. POTTERY
AND PORCELAIN

AMERICAN ceramics of the Victorian Period not only followed the rococo and neo-classical styles of European ceramics but modelers and decorators from English potteries came as émigrés to America and their influence dominated the ceramic industry in the United States in the nineteenth century. Stoneware, various kinds of earthenware, including the sgraffito ware of Pennsylvania, and even porcelain had been manufactured in various parts of America before 1840 and these wares continued to be made all through Victorian times, but certain other wares such as Parian, Majolica and Belleek, were first made in the nineteenth century and are distinctly Victorian not only because of their material, but because of their shapes and naturalistic and romantic designs which followed the trend of the decorative art of the period. As the period progresses we see exotic influences of Japan and Egypt. Persian and Moorish shapes and Renaissance designs also dominate certain ceramics.

In this period American ceramic manufacturers not only supplied the utilitarian needs of the people, but also began to compete with the European potteries in making the finest porcelains and art wares. As the Victorian period opened in about 1840, the American Pottery

221

Company in Jersey City made blue transfer-printed wares similar to Staffordshire. A water pitcher and mugs with printed portraits of William Henry Harrison, a log cabin, an eagle, and the inscription "The Ohio Farmer" printed in black, were made for the presidential campaign of 1840. The best-known products of the American Pottery Company were the Rockingham hound-handled pitchers which were made after English models by Daniel Greatbach who joined the company in 1839. Stoneware pitchers with hunting scenes and an Apostle pitcher were also made here. These were marked "American Pottery, Jersey City" or "D. & J. Henderson, Jersey City," impressed in a circle. The name of the firm was changed to the Jersey City Pottery in 1845. Later, although the wares were of high quality, they were never marked but were sold to the trade for decorating. It is some of this ware that was decorated by the Lycetts and thus it has value today, but it is very scarce and very expensive.

Another important pottery at this time was operated by Charles Cartlidge, an English potter, at Greenpoint, New York. They made porcelain buttons, door plates and door knobs, candlesticks, and biscuit porcelain busts of Daniel Webster, Zachary Taylor, Chief Justice Marshall and Archbishop Hughes, modeled by Josiah Jones. This factory closed in 1856, but the work was carried on under the name Union Porcelain Works, and porcelain tableware and decorative pieces were manufactured. Karl Müller, a sculptor, designed the famous Century Vase with historical American scenes which was exhibited at the

Group of New Jersey pitchers. LEFT TO RIGHT. Relief steamship and fire engine, both Salamander Works, Woodbridge, N.J. c. 1838–1845; white pitcher with relief grapevine, Swan Hill Pottery, South Amboy, N.J. 1860–1867; brown pitcher with grape pattern, Congress Pottery, South Amboy, N.J. 1849–1854. (*The Henry Ford Museum*)

Centennial. He also designed a Liberty cup and a vase to illustrate Longfellow's poem, "Keramos." A series of statuettes, pitchers and busts of famous Americans were also designed by Müller. The well-known artist J. M. Falconer was also employed as a decorator of plates and plaques at the Union Porcelain Works. Since many of the pieces, including the Centennial Vase, have been found both decorated and undecorated, it would seem that the decorated vase was the work of the two men, both sculptor and decorator. A charming trillium flower-form vase upheld by a frog was also made at the Union Porcelain Works and a tea set with heads of an Indian and a Negro as finials

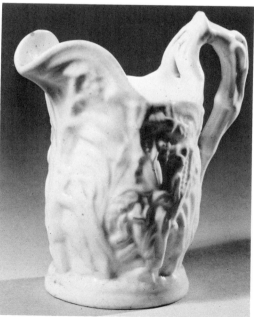

UPPER LEFT. Hound-handled pitcher, American Pottery Co.; Jersey City, c. 1845. (*The New-York Historical Society*) RIGHT. Rockingham pitcher inscribed "Protection to American Industry." (*The New-York Historical Society*) LOWER LEFT. Hound-handled pitcher, Jersey City, c. 1850. (*The Metropolitan Museum of Art*) RIGHT. Glazed porcelain pitcher, Charles Cartlidge & Company, Greenpoint, 1848–1856. (*The Brooklyn Museum*)

and squirrels and goats' heads as handles, was decorated with a rococo floral pattern and panels of birds and flowers. There were also vases with embossed gold and jewel work and grotesque lizards climbing up their sides. These are rare pieces, but since the works continued to the turn of the twentieth century many less important articles must be available. The factory used several marks, including an eagle's head grasping an "S" with "U.P.W." above, and "Union Porcelain Works, N.Y." impressed.

Fine porcelain was also made before 1900 by Kurlbaum and Schwartz of Philadelphia; Greenwood Company, Trenton, New Jersey; Bennett, New York; Lenox; Knowles, Taylor, and Knowles in East Liverpool, Ohio; and the United States Pottery Company in Bennington, Vermont.

The United States Pottery Company produced a great variety of wares—both pottery and porcelain, utilitarian and decorative. In fact, from 1847 to 1858 this pottery produced a vast output of wares. Under the direction of Daniel Greatbach, who had earlier worked at the Jersey City Pottery, such Rockingham ware designs as hound-handled jugs with grape designs and hunting scenes as well as with molded diamond and Gothic patterns were made. The six-sided brown pitcher with raised floral designs on the panels was made in at least four different sizes. The designs on the panels and the handle shapes

LEFT. Two pieces of toilet set of white graniteware decorated in blue and gold. RIGHT. Graniteware presentation pitcher decorated in gold and inscribed "U.S. Pottery Co/Bennington, Vt." (*The Henry Ford Museum*)

vary. These pitchers are marked "Norton & Fenton." Similar Rockingham ware pitchers were made by Ballard Brothers, and Nichols and Alford, in Burlington, Vermont, and by J. B. Caire & Co., Po'keepsie, New York, as well as in Ohio potteries.

Since most pitchers of Bennington Rockingham Pottery are scarce and expensive, it is best for the beginning collector to start with small utilitarian articles which are less in demand and therefore less expensive. There are mugs, tea and coffee pots, sugar bowls, pie plates, soap dishes, cuspidors, door-knobs, flowerpots, and picture frames. Of these articles, the most typically Victorian are the cuspidors and the picture frames. Bennington cuspidors were made in different sizes, shapes, and designs. The most common ones are those molded in panels with or without a diamond pattern. The flatter cuspidor with a clam shell design was also made in quantity. The rarer cuspidors are those with panelled columns or acanthus design. Some of the cuspidors are marked with the various 1849 stamps which include the date. Oval, round, square, and rectangular Rockingham picture frames with heavy moldings were made in many sizes at Bennington. They also made an elaborate rococo leaf pattern frame. These were not made at other factories. They are certainly distinctly Victorian, and are similar in design to the heavy walnut frames of the period.

Norton and Fenton paneled Rockingham pitchers with floral designs, 1845–1847 (*Bennington Museum*)

Besides the Parian ware which will be treated elsewhere, the molded pitchers with relief designs are the most characteristic Victorian forms. For the most part the designs and forms of these pitchers followed English leadership and many were exact reproductions of designs by Copeland, Minton, and other English potters. The "Cherub and Grapes" jug was copied from a Wedgwood design, and the "Good Samaritan," "Love and War" and "Pond Lily" jugs were also copies. "Bird and Nest," "Babes in the Woods," "Paul and Virginia" were also English adaptations. The only distinctly original American designs were the "Cascade" and "Corn" patterns. These elaborate relief designs are typically Victorian. They were molded in soft-paste porcelain, Parian and various other materials and cover almost every aspect of Victorian design. The jug or pitcher was on every middle-class Victorian table for use as a water or milk pitcher or as a jug for ale or beer, thus a great many of them were made. While a few of these patterns such as the Corn Husk are extremely rare, and any Bennington jug is rare, there are many small porcelain jugs from other American potteries which are available at less expensive prices.

Parian Ware

PARIAN is one of the most popular Victorian wares. It was first made by Copeland in England in 1842. Parian is a hard-paste unglazed porcelain that was designed for making cheap miniature reproductions of famous pieces of sculpture or portrait busts of celebrities, and was commonly called statuary ware or statuary porcelain. In texture and appearance Parian was a close approximation to Parian marble. Later, many pitchers, vases, boxes, and other small articles were made in Parian ware. English Parian is made mostly in the form of small statues. Statues and portrait busts were also made in American potteries, but the most collectible item is the Parian pitcher or vase.

Parian was made by Morrison & Carr in New York City and by the Southern Porcelain Company, Kaolin, South Carolina, whose products included a jug with an impressed wheat design and rustic

Group of Bennington Parian ware. TOP. Pitcher, Wild Rose pattern; blue and white vase, portrait medallion; water lily pitcher. BOTTOM. Eagle vase; figure of girl lacing shoe; rare blue and white pitcher, Cherub and Grape pattern. (*The Henry Ford Museum*)

handle. Ott & Brewer of Trenton, New Jersey, exhibited Parian vases and statues modeled by Isaac Broome, the sculptor, at the Centennial in 1876. In 1885 Parian wares were made at the Chesapeake Pottery. These included heads, flowers and medallions of Thorwaldsen's "Seasons" as well as original cattle-head plaques modeled by the sculptor James Priestman.

The first, and perhaps the best Parian ware produced in America was that made by the United States Pottery in Bennington. John Harrison, a modeler from Copeland, England, came to the United States Pottery to assist. At first, copies of English statuettes were made and it is difficult to distinguish similar pieces made by Copeland, Minton, Alcock, or other English potters from the American. Parian pitchers were made in the following designs; "Cascade," "Corn Husk," "Cherub and Grapes," "Cupid & Psyche," "Daffodil," "Good Samaritan," "Love & War," "Grapevine," "Pond Lily," "Snow Drop," "Tulip & Sunflower," "Wild Rose," "Bird & Nest," as well as a great many geometric, arabesque and vine designs. Tea sets, syrup jugs, mustard pots, and other tablewares were also made in Parian. This ware was also made in blue and white. The blue was painted on afterwards at most potteries but at Bennington it was mixed with the slip and baked.

Parian vases and fancy articles were not only molded with a design, but modeled decoration such as grapes, flowers, and rustic handles were added. Tall vases had portrait panels with grape and leaf decoration. There were also vases with panelled leaf designs and rare fancy cottage vases with panels of figures and applied molded handles of wheat, grapes or convolvulus. The "Ear of Corn" vase was a strictly American design and was made in various sizes. There were also vases

LEFT. Parian vase. Ceramic Art Company, Trenton, New Jersey, 1891. BELOW, LEFT. Parian pitcher, "Tulip and Sunflower." RIGHT. "Cascade" pattern, porcelain. Both pitchers made at U.S. Pottery, Bennington, Vermont. (*Bennington Museum*)

Parian vases with applied grape decoration. Hand, holding vase with molded fern design. (*Bennington Museum*)

with standing Victorian figures of a man or woman, cherub or small animal.

Perhaps the most popular vases with the collector today are the typically Victorian Hand vases. The hand is usually upright with a ruffled cuff and the vase a flower, leaf or shell form. These were made in several sizes. There were also vases in the form of flowers such as crocus or calla lilies and vases in the form of several kinds of shells. Another decorative Parian piece was the cologne bottle. These were made in rounded and square vase forms with molded panelled and fluted designs, and applied flowers and grapes. Covered jars and trinket boxes were also made in great quantities. These were made with molded decoration and applied flowers, grapes or molded cherubs, draped figures, dogs, ducks or lambs. The trinket box with the sleeping cherub is one of the most interesting.

There were also Parian busts and statuettes. Statuettes included the rare "Autumn," the "Greek Slave," after the sculptor Hiram Powers, and figures reminiscent of English Staffordshire cottage statues. There were also typically sentimental figures of children including the

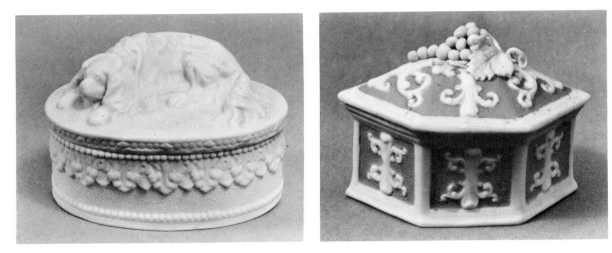

ABOVE AND BELOW. Parian trinket boxes with molded and applied decoration. (*The Metropolitan Museum of Art*)

"Praying Child," the "Tight Shoe," and "Red Riding Hood." The rare poodle carrying a basket was made in several sizes. Baskets and jewelry with applied flowers are also rare. For the collector of miniatures there were small vases, pitchers and toy tea sets. These, however, are rare.

The collector of American Parian Ware will want to own *Bennington Pottery and Porcelain* by Richard Carter Barret. Not only is it a guide to Bennington wares, but its photographs are a guide to types of Victorian pottery and porcelain produced in America in the last half of the nineteenth century and it gives a picture of the forms and designs which dominated the arts of the Victorian Age. How do you identify Parian? By its lack of glaze, by its form, and by its design. Few pieces are marked and it is almost impossible to differentiate between the American and English Parian.

Majolica

MAJOLICA was one of the most popular wares of Victorian times and it is also popular with collectors today. The majolica of the nineteenth century is a crude earthenware with molded relief designs. It is decorated with brilliant and often gaudy color by applying colors mixed with the glaze, green being a favorite. It was Minton in England who really started the craze for Victorian majolica when they exhibited their majolica at the London Exhibition in 1851 and in Paris in 1853. American potteries were quick to imitate the ware. They copied the earlier cauliflower and pineapple teapots and molded leaf plates of Wedgwood, but they also copied the jardinières and plates with fans, kittens and wickerwork made by Minton. Majolica, as no other ceramic, reflected the ornate, gaudy, bad taste of the last half of the nineteenth century.

Typical majolica designs included rustic patterns of basketry and wooden-bound buckets. There were bamboo, corn, pineapple, and cauliflower tea and coffee pots with handles of rustic tree branches or rose stems with thorns. Popular patterns included the wild rose, lily pad and herons, cattails and cabbage leaves, begonia and fern leaves, all of which were molded on plates. There were also plates with raised designs of strawberries and grapes, molded fish, and shells. Syrup jugs, cuspidors, jardinières, mugs, covered boxes, cake baskets and celery vases, sardine boxes, butter dishes with cow finials and beehive honey dishes were among the many articles made. Majolica tea services and a large variety of ornamental pitchers, vases, compotes, centerpieces, and sardine boxes with fish finials on their covers were made by Carr and Morrison in New York City.

The majolica made by E. & W. Bennett of Baltimore includes the famous large fish pitcher with a light blue glaze and molded design of fish, lobsters and shells. Vases with grapevine designs and lizard handles, large pitchers, coffee pots and other pieces with blue, brown and olive mottled glazes, and large jardinières set on griffon legs were also made at this pottery. In 1850 they produced a majolica bust of George

ABOVE. Etruscan majolica platter, Sea Shell pattern. BELOW. Leaf dish, Griffin Smith & Hill, Phoenixville, Pa., 1881–1892. (*The Henry Ford Museum*)

Washington. These pieces were usually marked "E. & W. Bennett/
Canton Avenue/Baltimore, Md." Griffen, Smith & Hill of Phoenixville,
Pennsylvania, became widely known for their Etruscan majolica.
Compotes with dolphin supports, flower, shell, and jewel cups, as well
as the popular design of coral and seashells in delicate pinks, gray and
green, and leaf and fern designs were made at this pottery. A catalogue
of the pottery shows several types of leaf dishes which were produced
in autumn colors, plates with wicker borders, and fluted borders with
molded flowers. A wicker vase has a molded spray of oak leaves and a
leaf tray has sections to hold a sugar and creamer. The well-known
seaweed pattern was available in many different shapes including a tea
set, plates, and a berry bowl. Etruscan majolica is light in weight and
thin compared to other majolica. The mark was an impressed monogram "G.S.H." sometimes surrounded by a band with the words
"Etruscan Majolica." The monogram
alone is also used and sometimes
"Etruscan Majolica" impressed in a
horizontal line.

The Chesapeake Pottery in Baltimore made majolica which is called
Clifton Ware and marked "Clifton Decor
B" on crossed crescents with the monogram "D.F.H." in the center. Other
makers of American majolica include
Odell & Booth at Tarrytown, New York;
the Hampshire Pottery at Keene, N.H.;

Majolica pitcher, Morley & Co., Wellsville, Ohio,
1879–1885. (*The Brooklyn Museum*)

and the Faience Manufacturing Company at Greenpoint, L.I. The majolica of the latter company has no impressed pattern, but is dipped in colored glazes and has a streaked or marbled appearance. Majolica was also made at Evansville, Indiana; by Morley & Co., Wellsville, Ohio, in 1879; and at the Arsenal Pottery in Trenton, New Jersey. Majolica toby jugs from the Arsenal Pottery were exhibited at the Chicago Fair in 1893.

There is a great quantity of majolica on the market today and it is cheap. Even the majolica stand with its matching jardinière, a real Victorian horror, is again offered to the public. However, the majority of the pieces in the shops today are of English make. American-made majolica if marked, and especially the lovely seaweed pattern of Etruscan majolica, is much higher in price and harder to find.

Belleek

ONE of the most unique Victorian ceramics was the thin iridescent porcelain called Belleek. It was first made in Belleek, Ireland, and was manufactured in America by Ott and Brewer at the Etruria Pottery in Trenton, New Jersey, in the 1880's, under the direction of William Bromley Sr. from the Belleek factory in Ireland. Belleek porcelain has a translucent pearly glaze, and is almost as thin as paper. It was made in both useful and ornamental wares, many in shell and flower forms with delicate fluted surfaces with crimpled edges on bowls and vases. The larger vases are simpler in outline, but often have pierced necks, handles and feet, and elaborate covers. Some are decorated in enamels and gold. Ott & Brewer Belleek is usually decorated in delicate blue, pink, and green, combined with gold and sometimes silver. The mark on Ott & Brewer Belleek is a crown pierced by a sword with Belleek above and "O&B" below. This is printed in red on top of the glaze. Another mark was a crescent with "Trenton" and "O&B" with "Belleek" above and "N.J." below. This was printed in red or brown over the glaze.

William Bromley also supervised the making of Belleek at the Willets Manufacturing Company. Many of Willets' forms were reproductions of the shell and coral forms of Irish Belleek, but some were decorated with delicate floral Dresden patterns. Small picture frames with molded flowers and porcelain clock cases were also made. One of the most beautiful pieces was the shell and cupid jug. This piece was also made at Ott & Brewer. The mark on Willets Belleek is a snake coiled to form a "W" with "Belleek" above and "Willets" below. It is printed in red on top of the glaze. In 1889 the Ceramic Art Company was founded by Jonathan Coxon Sr. and Walter S. Lenox, who had learned the process of manufacturing Belleek when employed at Ott & Brewer. In addition to table pieces such as the lily-shaped "Engagement" cup and saucer, they made vases with carved designs and a delicate swan dish. The mark on their Belleek is a graceful "C.A.C." within a circle, with an artist's palette and brushes above at the left, and the word "Belleek" printed in red below this stamp over the glaze. The Belleek swan dish is still made by Lenox. Other companies in New Jersey that manufactured Belleek were the American Art China Works of Rittenhouse, Evans & Co.; and Morris and Willmore.

Belleek dessert set, Ott & Brewer, Trenton, New Jersey, c. 1880. (*The Newark Museum*)

Lotus ware bowl. Knowles, Taylor & Knowles, Co. East Liverpool, Ohio, 1891–1898.

Oval ribbed dish, Willets Manufacturing Co., Trenton, New Jersey, c. 1890.

Cups and saucers, Belleek porcelain, Ott and Brewer, c. 1882–1894. (*The Henry Ford Museum*)

The latter marked their Belleek with a shield enclosing the interlaced letters "MW" with "Belleek" above and "Trenton, N.J." below. A small quantity of Belleek was also made by E. & W. Bennett and Belleek was also made at Bennington.

A considerable amount of Belleek china was made at Knowles, Taylor and Knowles in East Liverpool, Ohio, in the 1880's. Later they developed a similar ware known as "Lotus Ware." This was decorated in dainty colors and had openwork effects and raised gold borders in Renaissance style. The shapes were often oriental, but the decoration favored was cupids and butterflies. Each piece was an individual design. "Lotus Ware" was probably the finest porcelain made in America. The mark was "Knowles, Taylor and Knowles" in a circle surrounding a star and crescent and "Lotus Ware" beneath the circle. Another mark on their art ware was the initials of the company above the word "China." Lotus Ware is very expensive and is sought by museums, so there is little for the collector. The Belleek of the New Jersey potteries is available and the Lenox swans, salts and other

Belleek cup and saucer, Mercer Pottery Co., Trenton, New Jersey, c. 1876. (*The Brooklyn Museum*)

Belleek pitcher made by Walter Scott Lenox, 1887. This cupid design was also available for amateur hand-painters at Willets Manufacturing Company. (*The Newark Museum*)

BELOW LEFT. Lotus ware vase. Knowles, Taylor & Knowles. (*The Brooklyn Museum*) RIGHT. Lotus ware vase with hand-painted decoration. (*The Henry Ford Museum*)

delicate pieces are still being made as is Irish Belleek with green shamrock designs. Belleek baskets with roses on the rim are also still being
made. Since both the Irish Belleek factory and Lenox continue making
Belleek, this new Belleek is available, but pieces of old Belleek are difficult to find.

Art Pottery

ANOTHER phase of ceramics which developed in the Eighties was that
made by the artist-potter who created original designs and returned to
hand production. Through the influence of William Morris, Lewis Day
and Walter Crane in England new forms and new methods were introduced. The most famous American pottery that was an outgrowth of
this movement was the Rookwood Pottery in Cincinnati. The interest
started in a class of china painters and developed mainly through the
unique artistry of M. Louise McLaughlin who was not only a china
painter but also a ceramist. Her famous Losanti Ware, a hard-paste
porcelain, was exhibited in Paris at the Exposition Universelle in 1879
and a short time afterwards she organized the Pottery Club of Cincinnati.
A wealthy and influential member of this club, Mrs. Maria Longworth
Nichols (Storer), founded her own pottery and named it Rookwood. The
first kiln was fired in 1880. In the beginning, the pottery specialized in
breakfast and dinner services and other useful articles in cream color
or underglazed printed decoration of birds, fish and animal subjects.
These printed wares were gradually superseded by more artistic forms
in the Japanese manner and original work took the place of copying. The
shape of the vases and the naturalistic motifs, however, are distinctly
oriental in feeling. The vases were modeled on a potter's wheel, then the
unbaked piece was painted with colored slip, then fired. The vase was
then decorated, dipped and fired again.

There are several types of Rookwood which are distinguished by
their color and glaze. The regular or standard ware has an orange and
green glaze of which the corn design mug is an example. The mahogany
was a red and brown glaze. The sea green glaze was used with designs

of fish while the Iris glaze in soft blues and greens with suggestions of pink and green was used on Poppy, Rose, and Iris vases. There was also a mat glaze without gloss and the beauty of this type is in its texture. However, the Tiger's eye and gold stone, in which gold glistens through the dark glaze, is the highest achievement of the Rookwood pottery. According to Barber, the distinguishing feature of all of the varieties of Rookwood is the tinting and blending of the grounds beneath the heavy transparent colored glazes, which produces the effect of rich tones of black, yellow, red, olive, green, brown, and amber of great brilliancy, mellowness, depth, and strength.

The designs on Rookwood vases include White Lilac, Water Lilies, Goldenrod, Trailing Arbutus, Snowberry (orange), Maple, Spanish Chestnut, Chrysanthemum, Primula (red), Lily of the Valley, Poppies, Clover, Orchids, White Roses, Thistles, Pine Cone and Mushrooms. There were also designs with fish, geese, sea gulls, grasshoppers, eagles, dragon, and white storks. The Rookwood decorations are under the glaze. A 1904 catalogue illustrates many vases in color and quotes prices. The

Rockwood pottery. Dark vases mahogany glaze. Center vase chrysanthemum pattern. (*Dr. and Mrs. Robert Koch*)

Group of Rookwood pottery vases. LOWER CENTER. Dogwood design. RIGHT. Lily leaves. (*Dr. and Mrs. Robert Koch*)

Iris glaze designs of Poppy, Rose, Orchid and Iris were priced at $100.00 each, while the White Storks, Dragon and Geese designs were $100.00 to $250.00, according to size. Lamps with Tiffany glass shades were priced at $100.00. However, no two pieces were alike. Early designers besides Mrs. Maria Longworth Nichols (Storer) were E. P. Cranch, William McDonald, Matt A. Daly, Albert R. Valentien, Artus Van Briggle and Kataro Shirayamadani. An eagle vase decorated by A. R. Valentien and a dragon vase by Shirayamadani are among the early pieces and are in the Philadelphia Museum of Art. The Hollyhock design is also by Valentien. An Indian head design is by Van Briggle and a Standing Indian is by Grace Young. All Rookwood vases are marked, dated, and numbered for shape; lettered for size and color, and monogrammed by the decorator. The marks are as follows: 1880–82—"Rookwood Pottery Ohio" painted under the glaze. Also a rare "Rooks & Kiln" mark. 1882–86—"Rookwood" and year in rectangle—Impressed. 1886—"R.P." monogram with symbol for date. 1887—"RP" with one flame. One flame is added each year. This mark is still in use and a limited amount of the pottery is still being made. Rookwood Pottery is not an antique, but it will soon be, and such is the beauty of design and workmanship that it is well worth collecting. Since it was never produced in great quantities and since every piece is unique and signed, its value is bound to increase. Indeed, it was never cheap and continues expensive today.

Other art potteries of the nineteenth century which produced similar wares were the Newcomb Art Pottery at Biloxi, Mississippi; the Weller Pottery in Zanesville, Ohio; the Pauline Pottery of Edgerton, Wisconsin; and the Lonhuda Pottery Co. in Steubenville, Ohio. Among the decorators of Lonhuda Pottery was Miss Laura A. Fry of Cincinnati. The ware was marked "Lonhuda" with the monogram of the company and sometimes an impressed Indian head.

The Dedham Pottery which started as the Chelsea Ceramic Art Works, founded by Alexander Robertson in 1866, was another art

Dedham pottery plate, Crab design—crackle glaze. Stamped on bottom in blue square enclosing rabbit below, Dedham/Pottery.
(*The Henry Ford Museum*)

pottery. Through the years they made a variety of wares from reproductions of Greek vases and sculptured vases and plaques with illustrations of La Fontaine's Fables to experiments with Chinese sang de boeuf. This latter ware was the most successful, but the product that finally caught the response of the public was the gray crackle ware which was made after the works were moved to Dedham in 1896 where the business was carried on by Hugh Robertson. Dedham Ware has a porcelain body of hard fine quality with a soft grey crackle which is decorated with patterns of in-glaze blue. It is made completely by hand so that the pieces are often uneven. It is fired at a heat of 2,000 to 2,500 which gives it a softness of line and quality of color and makes the delicate tracery of the crackle which is suggestive of Chinese and Japanese pottery. At first the forms included vases and fruit and salad plates, but as the demand grew more pieces were added. The designs are conventionalized and look like stencils. Patterns include flowers such as hawthorn, fleur-de-lis, thistle, azalea, clover, horse chestnut, iris, and water lilies. Animals include rabbits, swan, owls, lion, turkey, ducks, turtles, elephant and polar bear. Other patterns were lobster, crab, dolphin, butterflies and a rare Birds in Orange Tree. These patterns were made in tableware including plates and tea sets. They also made flower holders, knife rests, coasters, boots and a bunny paperweight. Several well-known artists as well as students from the Art Museum School made the designs. The most popular pattern is the rabbit. The elephant is one of the rarest patterns. The marks changed every few years. The familiar mark was a rabbit with the words Dedham Pottery above.

Tea cup and saucer, Rabbit pattern. Stamped Dedham/Pottery with rabbit. (*The Henry Ford Museum*)

Another art pottery was made by Grueby Faience Company which was established in Boston in 1897. The pottery was a hard semi-porcelain, smooth and satiny, and had an opaque, lusterless enamel mat glaze. The colors were green, yellow and blue-purple, the decoration in low relief, Egyptian-inspired in plant forms of a slender plantain leaf and bud on a long stem. These were modeled by women artists who signed their monograms in addition to the impressed mark of the pottery which was "Grueby;" "Grueby Pottery, Boston, U.S.A.;" or "Grueby, Boston, Mass." This pottery was sold at Tiffany and Tiffany glass shades were first fitted on Grueby Pottery lamps. When the Grueby works closed Tiffany began to make his own pottery lamps.

Tiles

THE present-day destruction of many old nineteenth century mansions brings to the antique market various articles used in the decoration of these houses such as ironwork, carved mantelpieces, newel posts and stairways, and old tiles used on floorways, wainscoting and around fireplaces. Decorators have been collecting old ironwork and carved marble mantels, and museums are collecting architectural columns, figures and decorative panels, but old tiles have generally been neglected. The majority of the tiles were made commercially and the shiny majolica ones particularly are looked upon with scorn, but as our collecting outlook gradually broadens to take in the whole of the nineteenth century, no item, however small or unimportant, should be neglected.

Tiles were a popular type of decoration in the late nineteenth century. It was the influence of Eastlake and the exhibits of tiles at the Centennial that brought the production and use of tiles to the fore in both commercial and household decoration in America. Eastlake recommended the use of tiles not only around the fireplace and mantel, but as wainscoting and decorative insets on furniture. Minton produced a set of fireplace tiles with woodland plants and also furnished blank tiles for decorators in the 1880's. The *Art Amateur* illustrated several complete sets of fireplace tiles with designs of flowers springing from vases and gave complete directions for their painting.

The painting of single tiles was usually the first lesson in china painting for amateurs. In books of handiwork for ladies many uses for hand-painted tiles were suggested, including framing tiles to hang or use as teapot rests, tile screens, and fireplace tiles. In the last chapter of *Pottery and Porcelain of the United States* (1893 edition), Barber writes about tiles for decorative effect and he suggests framing art tiles and illustrates tiles with elaborately carved frames. He also suggests attaching tiles to the woodwork of the mantel, vertical tiles on each side and a horizontal tile across the top.

There were many well-known artists and potters who made tiles. In 1877 the famous Tile Club was organized by a group of New York artists. They met at each other's studios for food and recreation, but they also each decorated a tile. The tiles were cream-colored glazed Spanish tiles, eight inches square, and the decoration was usually in "Victorian blue" monochrome. A tile by Winslow Homer, one of the members, is still in existence. Tiles were also made by several of the so-called art potteries. E. P. Cranch decorated several sets of mantel tiles for Rookwood. One set illustrated the ballad of Isaac Abbott and another that of Giles Scroggins' Ghost. Rookwood also made other decorative tiles with floral decoration in the oriental manner. Tiles were also made of Dedham Pottery. Tiffany made glass tiles and used them for fireplace decoration. None of these tiles was made commercially and up into the 1880's the interest in tiles was mainly among artists.

However, the Low Art Tile Works in Chelsea, Mass. had been making tiles since 1877 and in 1883 under the title of J.G. & J.F. Low they produced tiles commercially for mantel facings, panels and stoves. The talented artist Arthur Osborne originated the designs which included heads, mythological subjects and animal, bird, and floral studies. They also made calendar tiles and tiles for place cards for the Papyrus Club in Boston, and the Decennial Dinner of the Lotus Club in New York. These latter were 4 inch tiles with a green glaze and a relief design of an Egyptian figure and a vase of conventional lotus flowers. In 1884

Low put out a catalogue of their tiles. The designs included flowers, leaves, geometric designs and decorative heads showing Egyptian, Greek and Japanese influence. The separate tiles of the designs were made to fit together to use in plaques, panels or fireplace facings. Flower designs included graceful designs of Japanese quince, apple blossoms, daisies, buttercups, mistletoe and wild roses. There were also designs of birds and bamboo, birds and berries, and marguerites and butterflies. Renaissance heads, dolphins and Greek vases, horses and chariots were classical designs. There was also a pastoral plaque of Pan with pipes, and a series of Seasons with winged cherub and inscriptions. One panel had the words "Tempus Fugit" and a design of cherubs while another pattern was labeled "The Revel." These designs were pressed in the clay, but in the high-relief tiles the undercutting was done by hand after the design had been stamped in the press. In *Century Magazine,* November, 1886, J.G. & J.F. Low advertised a book *Plastic Sketches* which contained a series of 47 bas relief designs. The book was satin covered and sold for $7.50. They also offered a free colored print of Low's Art Tile Stove.

Many commercial tile companies also made art tiles and almost every tile company employed an artist to make their designs. Companies producing encaustic or inlaid floor tiles also made relief tiles. Among these companies were the American Encaustic Tiling Co. of Zanesville, Ohio, who employed the modeler Herman Müller. His designs included pictures and portraits in relief, and panels of women and children in landscape surroundings. Also among his designs was a panel of "Swallows." When the company's enlarged works were dedicated in 1892, 15,000 souvenir tiles were given away. Today these tiles would be collector's items. The United States Encaustic Tile Company in Indianapolis, Indiana, also produced decorative tiles including a series of three mantel tiles, Dawn, Midday and Twilight.

Isaac Broome, well-known for his modeling at several New Jersey potteries, was also a modeler and designer at the Providential Tile Works, the Trent Tile Company in New Jersey, and the Beaver Falls Art Tile Company in Pennsylvania. His tiles included a head of Sappho and a series of panels representing Music, Poetry and Painting. He also did a panel of passion flowers, and portrait heads including one of Washington. The designer at the Cambridge Art Tile Company in Covington, Kentucky, was Ferdinand Mersman, formerly of the Rookwood Pottery.

The well-known artist, Charles Volkmar, was also interested in tile work as well as pottery, and in 1888 was a partner in the Menlo Park Ceramic Company and later the Volkmar Ceramic Company. He made tiles in Romanesque style for the decoration of buildings and private homes. These were made in great quantities, and if found today they are worth collecting for their excellent design and beautiful coloring of old ivory, pale blue and light maroon. Some tiles were also finished in old ivory and gold. There were also tile portraits of such well-known persons as President Benjamin Harrison, Grover Cleveland, and other celebrities, made at the C. Pardee Works in Perth Amboy, N.J. As well as being hand-painted, inlaid and decorated with relief patterns tiles were also printed. Many of these printed tiles were made late in the century as souvenirs of such places as Niagara Falls, Plymouth Rock, and Salem and were printed with local scenes.

BELOW. White earthenware tile with pink glaze showing cupids with musical instruments. Providential Tile Works, Trenton, New Jersey, c. 1895. RIGHT TOP. Tile, olive-green glaze, head of U. S. Grant, Trent Tile Works, c. 1885. BOTTOM. Tile, head of man with beard. J. & J. G. Low Tile Works, 1887–1888. (*The Brooklyn Museum*)

Crazy quilt of pieced blocks with appliqués of animals and figures. Made by member of the Haskins family, Granville, Vermont, c. 1875. (Shelburne Museum)

VII. LADIES' HANDIWORK

THE Victorian lady was continually busy with "art recreations," the name given to all sorts of Victorian fancywork. Every article of the household was considered worthy of decoration with gilt, paint, or needlework. Shell work, feather work, moss and wax work, and even taxidermy occupied the leisure of the Victorian lady. There were general books on handiwork including Mrs. Pullan's *Lady's Manual of Fancy Work; Ladies' Handiwork of Fancy and Ornamental Work* by Florence Hartley; *Art Recreations* by Levina Urbino; and *Woman's Handiwork in Modern Homes* by Constance Cary Harrison. There were also directions and patterns in the issues of *Godey's Lady's Book*, and there were separate books devoted to each type of handiwork. Mrs. Urbino lists some of the types of handiwork in *Art Recreations*. Included is shellwork, conework, potichomania, transparencies, leaf impressions, wax work, leather work, moss work, feather work, hair work, and taxidermy. Mrs. Pullan lists the following articles of handiwork as "suitable for presents": antimacassars, bags, book marks, suspenders, bracelets of crochet or bead work, cigar cases embroidered or crocheted, cushions, doilies, foot muffs, lambrequins, music cases, ottomans, and foot stools of Berlin Work, transparent illuminated painting or enamelling on glass; decorated

249

chessboards, screens, panels for doors or furniture. Indeed, the aim seemed to be to leave no article of domestic use undecorated.

Needlework

TODAY quantities of these ornamental articles have been taken out of the attic and are popular with present-day collectors and museums. Fine needlework has been an occupation of women for many centuries. Until the 19th century worsted work was an aristocratic pastime. The designs were conventionalized forms and the results depended upon the individual's artistic ability. When this work was taken up by a growing number of people, many without taste, patterns had to be devised as aids, and these were produced by a Berlin print seller. The patterns were at first engraved and hand-painted on paper, later they were stamped in color on canvas. The resulting work done in wool stitches was called Berlin Work. The patterns included flowers, fruit, parrots, deer, horses, leopards, dogs, cats, and other animals. The favorite Victorian dogs—the spaniel, Newfoundland, pug, and greyhound and the tabby cat were motifs for cushions and footstools.

Berlin Work carpet bag.
(*Museum of the City of New York*)

Berlin Work. Cat with border of grape leaves. (*The Index of American Design*)

In addition to the articles of household usage personal articles such as railroad bags, tobacco bags, glass cases, suspenders, and pin-cushions were made. Book marks and mottoes were also made in great quantities. Large mottoes framed in rustic walnut frames hung in every household. The inscriptions read: "Welcome," "Home Sweet Home," "What is Home without Mother;" "The Old Oaken Bucket;" "Simply to Thy Cross I Cling;" "Peace Be Unto You," and other such religious and homey sentiments.

One of the most interesting branches of this handiwork was the needlework picture. Copies of landscape, Biblical scenes and portraits as well as sentimental pictures of children and animals were popular subjects in Berlin wool work pictures of the mid-nineteenth century. Favorite pictures included "Mary Queen of Scots," "Washington Crossing the Delaware," "Scottish Chieftain," "The Sicilian Maid," "Byron at the Seashore," "Laertes and Ophelia," and portraits of Benjamin Franklin, Queen Victoria, George Washington and Napoleon.

LEFT. Beaded cushion with eagle and flags, c. 1870. (*The Index of American Design*) RIGHT. Beaded wall pocket, shoe shape. (*The Henry Ford Museum*)

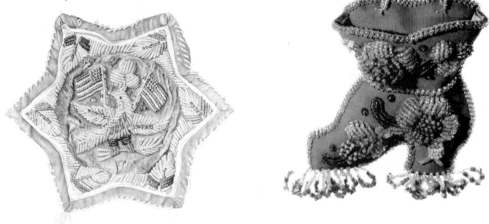

Wool embroidery on hair cloth. Walnut frame with gilt liner, 1875-1900. (*The Henry Ford Museum*)

Godey's, Peterson's, and Graham's magazines also illustrated patterns for beadwork wall pockets, watch cases, needle books, pen wipers, and pincushions. A piece of flannel was cut in the desired shape and the design cut in paper. The beads were strung and then sewed onto the paper pattern. Then this was sewed to the flannel. Designs included a flower spray, a leaf or a bird. Similar beadwork articles were made by the Tuscarora Indians and sold as souvenirs at Niagara Falls in the 1890's. The Indian work is usually backed with shiny cotton cambric, while the homemade articles utilized left-over materials from the scrap bag. Also, since Godey's and other magazines were printing directions in 1859, the ladies' work was older than that made by the Indians. A close examination and comparison would also show a difference in the quality of the beads. Other ladies made Berlin beadwork lambrequins, cushions and pincushions embroidered with chenille and pearls.

Lambrequins and antimacassars were also made of knotted twine called macramé, as well as in crochet or crazy-quilt work. Embroidered draperies and portières for doorways were made of intricate stitchery

Needlework scene New York from Weehawken, by Ann Stebbins, age 10, 1830–40. (*Collection of author*)

and elaborate floral designs. Patterns for these were illustrated in the *Art Amateur*, and exhibitions included a class of this type of needlework. Women also did a great deal of ecclesiastical needlework. Silk and gold thread geometrical and floral symbols were embroidered on the Burse and Veil, the Lectern hanging, and the minister's stole.

Shell, Feather and Wax Work

SHELL work was another fashionable occupation. The shells could be picked up at the seashore, or purchased at a store with directions for their use. Shell work bouquets, some of them charming, were made to

White feather wreath on black velvet ground. Walnut frame with gilt liner, 1850–1875. (*The Henry Ford Museum*)

fit into ornamental vases and set under glass domes for mantel garnitures. Others were made into pictures and framed. Feathers, cut into the shapes of flower petals and leaves, painted or dyed, were also made into bouquets and wreaths. Similar arrangements were made of beadwork, spun glass, and even mosses, dried leaves, pine cones, rice, beans and seeds. Small trinket boxes of shell were made in many whimsical forms. These were fastened to a cardboard foundation with plaster of Paris. These shell miniatures include such forms as slippers, cottages, tiny bureaus, boxes, and stars. There were also shell frames for pictures and clocks, and shell work animals.

In 1850 wax work, which had been popular in the eighteenth century, was revived, but instead of portraits and figures, arrangements

Wreath of seeds. Pine frame covered with gesso. 1865–1885. (*The Henry Ford Museum*)

of wax flowers and fruits were made. The *Handbook for Modelling Wax Flowers* furnished patterns and directions for modelling the fruit and flowers. Molds were available for larger pieces such as animals and birds. The fruit was usually arranged in a plaster of Paris basket and framed or set under a glass dome. Favorite flowers for wreaths or vases were orange blossoms, passion flowers, lilies, convolvulus, and fuchsias. In the Great Exhibition of 1851 a whole section was devoted to wax flowers which were considered not merely a craft but an important art form.

Painting on Various Materials

FLOWER painting on paper, canvas or silk was another popular recreation. It was taught in the schools and became a necessary accomplishment of every young lady of standing. Those who could not draw were taught with theorems or stencils. Painting on silk and velvet by means of stencils began early in the nineteenth century. It was applied to

Hand-painted silk fan. Tiffany & Co., 1873. (*The Newark Museum*)

velvet pictures, fire screens, chair cushions, and bell pulls. Painting was also done on linen, tapestry, canvas and mirrors. Later, flowers were painted on satin fans and fan painting became popular in the 1880's. Designs and directions for silk fan painting appeared in the *Art Amateur* in 1887 and 1889. Fans were painted on satin, silk, paper and vellum.

TOP. Painting on velvet, c. 1840. (*The Index of American Design*) BOTTOM. Landscape with woman. Painting on velvet, c. 1840. (*The New-York Historical Society*)

Basket of fruit. Painting or stencil on velvet, c. 1840. (*The New-York Historical Society*)

Black satin was painted in grisaille or monochrome in black, grey, and white. Designs included garlands of roses, violets, convolvulus, cyclamen, orange blossoms, jasmine and lilac. Pastoral scenes from Watteau, temple ruins, cupids and amorini from Boucher were also popular, as were oriental-inspired designs of birds, birds' nests, flowers and butterflies. Flowers were also painted on glass and the background filled in with opaque paint and crushed tin foil. These are collected as primitive

Towel-rack with hand-painted wild roses on tin, c. 1880. (*The Henry Ford Museum*)

paintings as are the paintings on velvet. Many of the paintings on velvet and plush were made in the 1880's when women were also painting plush picture frames. They also painted scraps of pieced work for crazy quilts. Hand-painted flowers also decorated black lacquer plaques, wall pockets, letter racks, and card trays.

Hair Work

MEMORIAL rings and medallions were made by artists and jewellers of the eighteenth century, but hair work for the amateur did not become the fashion until the mid-nineteenth century. In 1840, *The Jeweller's Book of Patterns in Hairwork* was published in London and in 1859 Godey's *Lady's Book* printed directions for hair work. In 1864 *Peterson's Magazine* included more instructions and the craze for hair work was launched and became fashionable until the end of the century. Bracelets, earrings, necklaces, pins, cuff links and shirt studs were made at home and taken to a jeweller for mounting. The interest in hair work began as an attempt to preserve a sentimental treasure. Brooches and lockets and woven chains contained the hair of a departed relative or friend and were worn as a sentimental memento or as mourning jewelry. Other articles were made by braiding and interlacing hair over hollow forms which included hearts, crosses, flowers, fruit and birds. Small charms for bracelets included fish, bird cages, horseshoes, chairs, teapots and other trinkets similar to those worn on charm bracelets today. Hair wreaths, bouquets and pictures were also made and framed to hang on the wall and hair was used in embroidery work. There were hair albums containing locks of hair of relatives and friends, and hair genealogical family trees set under glass domes were high fashion in the 1860's and 1870's.

Memorials of a tombstone, weeping willow and a mourning figure had been popular since the early nineteenth century and these continued to be painted, embroidered or cut in paper until the end of the century.

Hairwork jewelry from catalogue of A. Bernhard & Co., 1870.

Wood Carving and Fretwork

WOOD carving, which has been neglected by both writers and collectors of Victorian antiques, was considered one of the important art recreations in the last half of the nineteenth century. There were manuals of wood carving and articles giving patterns and instructions ran in several magazines including the *Art Amateur* in the 1880's and 1890's. The important promoters of wood carving were Charles G. Leland, Director of the Public Industrial Art School in Philadelphia, and author of *A Manual of Wood Carving*, and Benn Pitman of the Cincinnati School of Design. William H. Fry also conducted a carving school in Cincinnati. While the average wood worker carved small boxes, trays, plaques, and wall brackets, the pupils of Benn Pitman worked on more ambitious projects. There were 100 women in the first wood carving class organized by Benn Pitman in 1873 and among the articles carved were cabinets, chairs, church lecterns, screens, tables, doors and mantels.

Few of the smaller objects can be identified today but there are examples of mantels preserved in several houses in Cincinnati, chairs and church benches, and Benn Pitman's own house, which includes carved stairways, doors, mantels and a bed, is also preserved. Pitman's class of women, together with Mr. Fry, carved the panels of the organ in the Cincinnati Music Hall. They also carved an oak leaf frame for the portrait of Mrs. Hayes which once hung in the White House.

With a little search smaller items of wood carving such as flowers or portrait plaques, frames, wall brackets, boxes, trays, platters, bread trays, bellows, knife handles, and tankards should be found, especially in such cities as Cincinnati and Philadelphia where schools of wood carving were known to exist. The woods used included oak, walnut, cherry, maple, ash, white holly, and ebony. Designs for plaques included Spring, Summer, Autumn and Winter, portraits of women in peasant dress, animals such as birds, rabbits, dogs, cats and deer, and the favorite

Fretwork patterns for shelves and a hanging cabinet by A. H. Pomeroy, Hartford, Connecticut. (*The Century Magazine,* 1884)

Victorian flowers, wild rose, passion flowers, marigold, lilies, convolvulus and horse chestnut, grapes, oak and acanthus leaves. A favorite motif for the carved wall bracket was a stag's head with antlers, a dog's head, or dead game. Picture frames had a design of carved acanthus, ivy or oak leaves.

Fretwork, Sorrento carvings, or jigsaw work, was closely allied to wood carving and for those with less talent and perseverance, it presented an easier occupation. *Fret Cutting and Perforated Carving* by W. Bemrose Jr., was published in 1869. It gave patterns and directions for such articles as book rests, brackets, table mats, mirrors, card baskets, letter racks, envelope boxes, picture and mirror frames, table easels, hanging bookshelves, cupboards, corner brackets, bread platters, and finger plates for doors. Designs of ivy and oak leaves were combined with fretwork which was cut out with a small scroll saw. Sometimes the fretwork wall pockets and towel racks had panels of Berlin work em-

Designs for carved wood wall pocket and mirror frame by Benn Pitman. (*The Art Amateur,* 1888)

broidery. Fretwork was demonstrated in a booth at the Centennial and later commercial companies furnished designs. A. H. Pomeroy of Hartford, Connecticut, put out a catalogue of designs including a "Curfew" bracket showing a cut-out design of a woman ringing a bell, a card receiver with heron and cattail design, a grape design, and a shelf design of a farm scene with horses and chickens. A wall cabinet had an oriental design. Among the 500 designs offered for $2.00 by Adams & Bishop of New York was a cut-out portrait of President Garfield. Other designs included leaves, scrolls, birds, flowers, and deer.

Charles G. Leland in articles in the *Art Journal* of 1886–1887 mentions other home arts such as gesso painting, shell and horn cutting on nautilus and oyster shells, mosaic powder-work, and pyrography or wood-roasting. Some of these articles are to be found in shops today. Although they are in bad taste, they are bought by decorators who use them to add a bizarre note to a room. They are collected by museums as part of the picture of another age. You, too, can collect them for the same reasons. They are found in second-hand shops, flea markets, and at country auctions.

Pieced, Appliqué and Crazy Quilts

QUILTING is centuries old. In Europe it thrived as a folk art among the peasants and country folk, but it also flourished in the castle as well as the cottage. Materials for quilts varied in different countries. In France, Italy and Spain silks, damasks, brocades, and velvets were used, while in England and the Low Countries the early quilts were of hand-woven linen or East India chintz. Quilting reached its height of popularity in Britain and the Low Countries in the seventeenth century when the English, Dutch, Swedes and French started their migrations to America. Here the art of quilting changed, acquired new vigor, and adjusted to the needs of the pioneer settlers. However, the national characteristics of each group remained imprinted on their quilts and today the quilts of New England differ from those of the Pennsylvania Germans or the Southern Mountaineers.

American quilts are a record of American life. The early Crazy Quilts depict the hardships of pioneer America and the struggle of the wives of early settlers. We get a picture of the social life in the simple recreation of the quilting bee. The materials of the quilts show us the fabrics and patterns of the clothing and the development of the American textile industry, beginning with the homespuns of the Colonies and later the cotton products of the mills in the South and in New England. Early quilts show the Far Eastern-inspired printed floral patterns of England or the French Toile de Jouy and later the small calico sprig designs of American manufacture. Above all else the quilt was a family record. There was a bit of grandmother's wedding dress, a piece of the dress Aunt Julia wore when crossing the plains, the printed cotton that

Appliqué coverlet showing blocks of various patterns. Mid-nineteenth century. (*The Metropolitan Museum of Art*)

Mother wore on the picnic when Father proposed and a piece of Baby's christening bonnet. The different periods of American history are also reflected in the quilt designs. Colonial quilts resemble those made in Europe, and Revolutionary quilts took on a French accent, but in the pioneer period when the West was being settled, quilts became distinctly American in design, material, and workmanship.

The Crazy Quilt is an American product. It was first made in colonial days when new materials were not available or were too expensive, thus the old quilt was patched with whatever material was at hand. It was usually an odd piece left over from a dress. These pieces were also saved to make a new quilt. In the pieced crazy quilt there was no planned pattern or color. Each piece was fitted together as in a picture puzzle. Pieces of wool were put together with linen or calico regardless of size or color. The "Hit or Miss" was the next step in quilt making. Pieces were cut in uniform size and shape, but were pieced together without regard for color or material. Next, colors were sorted and arranged in rows to make the "Roman Stripe" with alternating stripes of light and dark. Alternating squares of dark and light produced the "Brick Wall." Another one-piece design was the Honeycomb. Real design began with the use of the triangle, when the pieces were carefully cut out and pieced together according to a plan of color and design.

The simplest patterns were made up of different arrangements of the four-patch block. One of the simplest designs used in the nineteenth century was the nine-patch Checkerboard. The nine squares of varicolored materials were set on their points and alternated with squares of white muslin. When put together with small blocks the Nine-Patch Chain was made. There were many other variations of this simple square design and oblong patches were set together to form the Zig-Zag. Squares, circles, and triangles were the foundation of many other designs which were given such imaginative names as "Windmill," "Fox and Geese," "Pincushion," "Sunburst," "Star of the East," "Morning Star," and "Flying Birds." Another typical American nineteenth century design was the "Log Cabin." Narrow "logs" were fitted together about a center square. This design was especially popular after the Civil War. There were many geometric variations of this pattern such as "Courthouse Steps" and "Windmill Blades." These quilts usually had turkey-red center squares.

Other popular pieced-work quilt patterns were "Le Moyne Star," "Boxes," and the intricate "Star of Bethlehem" and "Wheel of Fortune." There are also a group of religious quilt patterns among the pieced quilt designs. These include the "Christian Cross," "Star and Cross," "Jacob's Ladder," "Job's Tears," "King David's Crown," "Crown of Thorns," "Garden of Eden," "Golden Gates" and "World Without End."

Sometimes pieced work was combined with appliqué. Appliqué quilts demand more expert workmanship, however, for the design must

Foundation Rose and Pine Tree, red calico with yellow and green. Third quarter 19th century. (*Shelburne Museum*)

first be cut, then turned and hemmed before the final process of appliqué. Although there are geometrical design appliqué quilts, the most popular designs were floral, and of all flowers the rose had top priority. There is the beautiful "Rose of Sharon" made of red and pink calico with green

Patchwork "crazy quilt" of velvet put together with various embroidery stitches. 1890–1900. (*The Henry Ford Museum*)

leaves and stems, " The Rose Wreath," "Cactus Rose," "Rose Tree," "Rose of Dixie," "Wild Rose," and dozens more. Other flower designs included the "Aster," "Bleeding Hearts," "Cockscomb," "Dahlia," "Daisy," "Poppy," "Lily," "Prairie Flower," "Sunflowers," and "Tulip." There were "Autumn Leaf," "Oak Leaf," and "Laurel Leaf" designs and "Christmas Tree," "Charter Oak," "Cherry Tree and Birds," and "Tree of Life." There were also many kinds of fruit designs and designs with birds and animals—some naturalistic and some geometric or symbolic. The basket group includes some of the most popular and decorative designs. There were "Basket of Daisies," "Basket of Oranges," "Rose Basket," "Tulip Basket" and "Grandmother's Basket."

Many quilts were named after people. These patterns include "Cleopatra's Puzzle," "Fanny's Fan," "Martha Washington Star," "Mrs. Cleveland's Choice," and "Peeny Pen's Cottage." Designs were also named after games and puzzles such as "Jack-in-the-Box," "Merry-Go-Round," "Puss-in-the-Corner" and "Tic-Tac-Toe." Especially interesting to the collector is the group of quilts made for special occasions such as the "Bridal Wreath" quilt which had hearts set in the well-known wreath design. "Wedding Ring," "Bridal Stairway" and "Game of Hearts" were other nuptial patterns. Usually these quilts were sewn at quilting parties held to announce the engagement of a happy pair.

Other quilts made by a group were the Friendship. Presentation, Autograph and Album quilts. They were made by exchanging quilt blocks among a group of friends. As the name indicated, they expressed admiration or friendship for a particular person and the presentation took place at a gathering where each block was presented, then assembled and stitched. Many of the blocks were signed with names embroidered, cross-stitched or written in indelible ink. Each block was different in design and no set pattern was followed.

Historical or political quilts are among the most interesting and valuable quilts for collectors. These included flag quilts with star and eagle emblems. These quilts can usually be dated by the number of stars. Such patterns as "Cleveland Tulips," "Garfield's Monument," "Harrison Rose," "Kansas Sunflower," "Peary's Expedition," "Tippecanoe and Tyler Too," "Union Star," and "Confederate Rose" have political implications. It is also possible to trace the pioneer trail westward by the various quilt names. "Road to California," "Prairie Lily," and "Log Cabin" tell the history of settlement. The westward move from state to state is also recorded in the names of quilt patterns. There was "Boston Beauty," "New Jersey Rose," "Ohio Beauty," "Indiana Rose," "Kansas Sunflower," "Kentucky Peony," "Missouri Star," "St. Louis Star," "Star of Texas," and "California Star." Many of these names are variations of the original star and rose patterns. Elizabeth Wells Robinson lists over a hundred star patterns and almost fifty rose pattern variations.

Two unique historical quilts made in the third quarter of the nineteenth century are in the collection of the Shelburne Museum. One is the Civil War counterpane which is a combination of pieced work and appliqué with figures of cavalry and foot soldiers, animals, and a figure cut from the ad of Baker's Chocolate. The Abraham Lincoln spread includes a block with a seated figure of Lincoln and a block showing the Lincoln-Douglas debate. There are also blocks with animals, flowers, a clock, a Bible open to Psalms 103 and 104 and a vase of flowers on a table. The quilt is signed and dated February 10, 1865.

Late in the nineteenth century the lowly crazy quilt was revived, but velvets and silks were used instead of cotton and wool and the quilt was used as a throw for the couch or a cover for the parlor table. The various shaped pieces of the quilt were fastened together with a variety of feather stitches in silk floss and even the centers of the patches were ornamented with fanciful embroidery flower sprays, fruits, hearts, horseshoes, fans, and hand-painted designs on plush. Although these silk crazy quilts took endless hours of work and some of them contain intricate stitchery, many have been relegated to the scrap bag, the Good Will or the Salvation Army. Today, however, they are being collected again and even displayed and used. If you have one, keep it.

After the designs were pieced or appliquéd the actual quilting was done. The purpose of the quilting is to hold the pieced or appliquéd quilt top to its back and lining. The simplest quilting consisted of vertical, horizontal, or diagonal lines. When diagonal lines crossed they formed a diamond pattern. Leaves, vines, and interlacing squares, diamonds, and circles are used as borders, and plain blocks and borders are filled with geometric squares and circles. Sometimes the design of the appliqué square such as a basket is repeated in the background quilted square. Quilting designs include shells, feathers, wreaths, harps, stars, birds, peacock feathers, doves, eagles and rosettes. Religious motifs such as crosses and patriotic symbols such as anchors, flags and Liberty Bells often appear in quilted backgrounds.

Collecting quilts can be a fascinating hobby, whether you are

Civil War quilt, chintz, Scotch gingham, calicoes on homespun linen backing. Colors brown, cream, blue, rose and dull reds. Third quarter 19th century. (*Shelburne Museum*)

looking for a few as covers for your antique beds or whether you are forming a collection. Quilts of the American Victorian period are a distinct form of American folk art. The majority of the patterns were originated by the American needlewoman, for the European influence had disappeared by the mid-nineteenth century. You can collect quilts for pattern, for color, or for beautiful handwork. Be sure the quilt is in perfect condition, unless it happens to be a historical quilt, where some wear and fading is permissible. Quilts that are signed or dated are also rare, as are friendship and autograph quilts. Appliqué quilts with intricate patterns of flowers or long slender lines such as the Mariner's Compass should be noted for good needlework. Quilts with elaborate quilted backgrounds are rare and expensive. Color as well as pattern is an important consideration in quilt collecting. Some quilts have such beautiful color combinations that the maker must certainly have been an accomplished artist working with the needle instead of the brush. You can find quilts in country antique shops and at country auctions. Quilts are still being made in rural districts and exhibited at county and state fairs so if you want a quilt and not necessarily an antique one, go to the fair!

Hand-Painted China

CHINA painting was among the accomplishments of the fashionable Victorian lady and if we are to judge from the literature on the subject, china painting had priority over such other fashionable handicrafts as hair work, needlework or leather work. The craze for china painting which was popular in England and the Continent from the middle of the nineteenth century did not become the vogue in America until some years later.

The first china painting classes in America were those taught by Edward Lycett, formerly of Staffordshire, England. He came to America and established a china decorating business in New York in 1861, where he employed thirty or forty people painting and gilding imported and some American porcelain wares. His first classes in china painting were organized in New York after the Civil War. Later Lycett taught classes at the St. Louis School of Design and in Cincinnati. He decorated some stoneware for a company in East Liverpool, Ohio, in 1879. He also decorated vases for the Jersey City Pottery. In 1884 Lycett joined the Faience Manufacturing Company of Greenpoint, Long Island, and assumed direction of the factory. He designed new shapes with richly embellished ornamentation and embossed and perforated work on the handles and foot. The shapes showed Persian and Moorish influence. Lycett's three sons were also china decorators at the factory and for many years were actively engaged in teaching china painting as well— William Lycett in Atlanta, Georgia; F. Lycett in Bridgeport, Connecticut; and Joseph Lycett in Brooklyn. An original vase by Edward Lycett is in the Henry Ford Museum, and a plate with game decoration is in the New-York Historical Society.

The second step in the development of china painting in America was taken in Cincinnati, Ohio, in 1875. Benn Pitman, the Director of the Cincinnati School of Design, organized a class in china painting which was taught by Miss Eggers, a German lady who had studied at Dresden. There were many talented women in this class, including M. Louise McLaughlin, whose pottery, when exhibited at the Centennial in Philadelphia and in Paris, won special recognition. From this successful class the interest in pottery and china painting spread rapidly and in a short time there were china painting classes in all big cities throughout the country. Young ladies' seminaries and art schools included china painting in their curricula, china painting was taught at Chautauqua, and by 1900 there were courses in china painting at the International Correspondence School. China painting clubs also sprang up all over the country. Indeed, china painting, which has been looked upon as perhaps the worst Victorian horror, was the most stylish attainment of the ladies of the gay nineties. Also, although china painting was an amateur accomplishment, it was treated with esteem and given serious approval, and even in the art world its acclaim was world wide. Exhibits of china painting were held in London (The First Annual Exhibition of China Painting in 1875); at the Centennial Exposition in Philadelphia in 1876; at the National Academy of Design in New York in 1878; at the Exposition Universelle at Paris in 1879; and at the Brussels Exposition in 1881.

RIGHT. Plate decorated with panels of game by Edward Lycett, c. 1877. (*The New-York Historical Society*) LEFT. Vase made for Edwin A. Barber by Joseph Lycett at Faience Manufacturing Co., Greenpoint, New York, 1889. (*The Henry Ford Museum*)

The first annual exhibition of china or mineral painting in America was held in Chicago in June, 1888.

China painting had thus not only become the craze but was also an accepted branch of decorative art. At least a dozen books on china painting were published in America and many more published in England were available in American shops from 1875 down into the twentieth century. The best-known books were by M. Louise McLaughlin of Cincinnati whose *China Painting: a Practical Manual* was published in 1878. Camille Piton, the Principal of the National Art Training School, also published *A Practical Treatise on China Painting in America* in 1878, and in 1888, A. H. Osgood, the Director of Osgood's Art School, published *How to Apply Royal Worcester, Matt, Bronze, La Croix and Dresden Colors to China*. The advertisement of the Osgood Art School which appeared in *The China Decorator* in 1888 gives considerable information about china painting in America at this time. Instruction was $1.00 for a three-hour lesson, six lessons for $5.00. The ad read as follows: "Mineral painting upon china—heads, figures, landscape, flowers. Royal Worcester, Doulton, Dresden methods. Fruit, fish, game. Pupils are supplied with original designs to copy from. (China fired daily. 5 kilns.) French and English china, also American Faience. Hand-colored Royal Worcester and Doulton decoration suitable for lamps, vases, plaques. Royal Worcester, Matt and Bronze colors. La Croix colors. Royal Dresden colors. Special directions for Fish. Twelve different designs." Mrs. Osgood also gives a few notes on the different kinds of china available for paintings. She recommends Berlin porcelain for figure painting and French porcelain for its general excellence. "Of English ware Copeland's (Spode) has a blue-white glaze. Minton's has a gray tone and Doulton is creamy—good for pinks and gold. American ware is beautiful and unique in forms for table and art pieces. Trenton Ware has a creamy glaze and delicate finish." Mustache cups and rose jars of Teplitz Ware from Germany were also available to amateur china painters.

The Book of the China Painter by L. Vance-Phillips, the teacher at Chautauqua, was published in 1896. In addition to the many books, *The China Decorator,* a magazine devoted to china painting, was published from 1887 to the end of the century and the *Art Amateur* (1879–91) also contained a section devoted to china painting.

In the 1870's the National League of Mineral Painters held competitions for designs for a government table service for state dinners. It would seem that this competition did not produce the desired designs, but it did create interest, for in 1879 Mrs. Hayes, wife of President Hayes, retained the New Jersey artist Theodore R. Davis to design shapes and water color studies for a complete set of china for the White House. These designs were of American flora and fauna, including corn, goldenrod, buffalo, wild turkey, a scene of Indians, Harvest Moon, Clam Bake and Clam Chowder, and a scene of the artist's studio in Asbury Park, New Jersey. An effort was made to have this china made at a New Jersey pottery, but when this could not be done in the time alloted, the china was made by Haviland in Limoges, France. A year later this china was reproduced by Haviland and sold in New York by Davis, Collamore.

Haviland china plates painted by Nellie Bonham Foreman of Charlotte, Michigan, c. 1891. (*The Henry Ford Museum*)

Any of these pieces are collector's items today. Mrs. Harrison, the wife of a later President, was herself an active china painter. Some of her original designs of corn and goldenrod were used on Limoges plates for the White House.

In general the shapes and designs of hand-painted china were typical of the era and had a definite Victorian flavor. Tops of bowls and lips of vases were crimped. Handles and feet of many vases were in the form of lion's heads and feet, grotesque masques or cupids, and many vases had handles and bases of ornate perforated work. Designs included cupids, veiled figures, and flowers in the Japanese manner. Persian, Moorish and Renaissance influences were also seen in both forms and decoration. Although patterns of Royal Worcester, Doulton, Wedgwood, Royal Vienna and Dresden were copied, many of these designs were beyond the talents of the average amateur, so that simpler designs of flowers, butterflies, birds and fruits were used. Violets, pansies, chrysanthemums, poppies, morning-glory, passion flower, cactus, wild roses, clematis and periwinkle were favorite flowers; cherries, grapes, peaches, currants, blackberries and gooseberries were popular fruits.

Sets of fish, game, fruit, and nut plates had appropriate designs. The fish set usually included various kinds of fish amid grasses, seaweed, shells and rocks. Fishing rods, creels and flies often completed the scene.

Salmon were reserved for the platter. The game set included different species of game,—redhead ducks, peacocks, wild geese, mallard ducks, clover pheasants, canvasbacks, woodcocks, partridge, snipe, teal, prairie chickens, with wild turkeys on the platter. Fruit plates would have various kinds of fruit in their centers. Sprays of leaves and nuts decorated nut plates, while the ice cream dishes were painted with winter scenes. The punch bowl usually was decorated with grapes and leaves. The bread plate had sprays of wheat, and for oatmeal there was a bowl and saucer decorated with oak leaves and acorns. *The Art Amateur,* 1889, contained an article on cupid designs after Boucher, and Amelia G. Austin in her series of articles in *Ladies' Home Journal* says: "No branch of mineral painting is more fascinating than the painting of cupids and tiny heads."

China painting is scorned today and rightly so, since pieces available are generally of the worst amateur variety. However, many of the teachers and designers were artists of ability who were recognized in the art world of their time. One of these was Charles Volkmar who had studied in Paris

LEFT. Porcelain vase, Knowles, Taylor & Knowles, painted by Harry R. Thompson, 1891–1898. (*The Henry Ford Museum*) CENTER. Vase with designs of landscape and cattle painted by Charles Volkmar, c. 1881. (*The Brooklyn Museum*) RIGHT. Covered pitcher with grotesque dragon handle and chrysanthemum decoration attributed to Joseph Lycett, Faience Manufacturing Co., c. 1890. (*The Henry Ford Museum*)

under Harpignies and others, and was known for his paintings of landscape and cattle. While in Paris, Volkmar became interested in the Limoges method of underglaze painting. He worked in one of the potteries to learn the secrets of the process. When he came back to America in 1879 he built a kiln in Greenpoint, Long Island, and manufactured vases and tiles. These were marked "Č." In 1895 Volkmar established the Volkmar Keramic Company. These products are decorated with underglaze blue designs of historical buildings and American portraits. They are marked "Volkmar" with raised letters. Later together with Kate Cory, Volkmar opened a pottery at Corona, New York, and the mark here was "Volkmar and Cory Crown Point Ware" impressed. Vases with plain green glazes were marked "V" in 1896. Later Volkmar was engaged in architectural work in the William Rockefeller Mansion in Tarrytown, New York, in the Boston Public Library, and also many other residences of prominent people.

In 1903 Volkmar established a works at Metuchen, New Jersey, and made tiles, lamps and umbrella stands. The patterns were made by the running of the glaze. There were sprays of foliage and decorative patterns on white grounds with glazed orange linings in the bowls. Tile designs included ducks, also tiles with designs of Dutch Windmills by Volkmar are shown in the *Book of the China Painter* by L. Vance-Phillips, and there are designs for a game service and for a fish service also by Charles Volkmar. These designs would surely be beyond the ability of the average amateur and if any such plates were found today they would undoubtedly be well executed and worth collecting. Since each design was signed perhaps they were engravings of actual pieces which Volkmar himself decorated.

Another artist of ability who taught china painting and furnished designs for amateurs was Camille Piton, the Principal of the National Art Training School. Some of Piton's designs together with directions for painting are included in the *Art Amateur* as supplements. These included the following plate designs: Morning-glories; Blackberries; Pink Azalea; Pyrus Japonica; Wild Roses and Wheat; Poppies, Daisies and Wild Asparagus; Horse Chestnuts and Dogwood; and Vesuvius in Eruption seen from the Amalfi Drive. Piton also furnished the designs for hand-painted plaques including the following subjects: Fair Yseult, Sarah Bernhardt, Le Bel Ysambeau, Fleur de Pommier, a Lady and Gentleman of the XVI century, and In the Greenwood. Especially interesting is the plate design of Corn and Squash. Original designs for plates and plaques by Georges Wagner were also illustrated. These included Chicks and Mushrooms, Bird and Willow, and Mouse and Wheat.

George Theophilus Collins was another china painter and teacher in New York, who had studied in both Meissen and Sèvres potteries. Collins' designs for vases, bowls, cups and saucers and chocolate pots were illustrated in *The China Decorator*. These designs included a bowl with raspberry design, a wisteria vase, poppy vase, chestnut, wheat and daisies, ferns, sweet peas, heliotrope, pussy willow and Easter lilies. A teapot with animal handle and spout and bird finial has a design of flowers and rococo shells and scrolls. E. Aulich, another New York china painting teacher who operated a shop for decorating lamp globes, also furnished designs illustrated in *The China Decorator*. In the 1900 issue a color supplement of his familiar design of white roses on a round lamp globe was included. A design for corn and wheat on a simple pottery jug was by H. W. Staradin who also furnished many other designs for *The China Decorator*. Louis Prang & Co. also made many colored chromos of plate designs for hand painting.

There were 20,000 professional china painters and probably twice that many amateurs in 1905. *The China Decorator* lists Franz A. Bischoff, a well-known artist of Detroit, together with Aulich, Marshall Fry, Miss Mason, Mrs. Leonard and Mrs. Robineau (Adelaide Alsop Robineau, who later became famous for her own pottery, started as a china painter) as the best china painters of the 1880's. Marshall Fry was a well-known New York decorator and W. A. Mason was an instructor at the Pennsylvania Museum School. A china painting design of holly by Mrs. Mason was illustrated in the *Art Amateur* January, 1887. Mrs. Leonard was from Cincinnati.

There are several different methods of china painting. The majority of the pieces of amateur china painting are done by the overglaze technique, that is, the painting is applied to the glazed surface that has previously been fired. The colors are then refired at a low temperature. Underglaze painting is done on the biscuit china before it is glazed. Colors are then applied and the surface fired with high heat. Underglaze is the oil painting of the ceramic artist.

The women of the Cincinnati Pottery Club used both overglaze and underglaze methods. Miss McLaughlin worked and taught the Limoges or pâte-sur-pâte method of painting the surfaces of unbaked pieces with colored slips. The colors mixed with clay and water were applied to the damp clay and water surface.

By far the largest American pottery which catered to the amateur china painter was the Willets Manufacturing Co. of Trenton, New Jersey. Under the title of "The Celebrated Willets' Art Porcelain For Amateur Decoration" many pages of illustrations of the various articles and shapes appeared in *The China Decorator* between 1887 and 1889. These included tea cups, after dinner coffee cups, bowls with crinkled edges, and vases with perforated handles, covers, and bases. There are also vases and bowls with rustic handles and stands and bowls and bottles of wicker design. A rustic tree trunk with acorns holds a cornucopia vase and another tree trunk vase has a basket and jug at its base. There are also interesting bamboo jugs and a bamboo teapot, sugar and creamer. A squat jug or pitcher has a fancy handle and a masque spout.

Vase made by Willets Manufacturing Co., c. 1880. Overglaze decoration by amateur china painter. (*The New-York Historical Society*)

However, the finest designs are those of shell or flower forms. There is a delicate three-inch water lily vase and a lily cup on its lily-pad saucer. A fluted shell compote stands on a rustic base decorated with small shells and there is a small 2½ inch shell vase on a stand and a larger 7½ inch shell jug with coral handle. The most graceful and important piece is the shell and cupid jug. This jug was illustrated as the colored supplement of *The China Decorator* in March, 1888, with a description of its color—pink, white, pale green and gold. The jug (9½" x 9½") in blank Belleek porcelain for decorating could be purchased for $12.00. A duplicate jug in the Newark Museum is marked "W.S.L. 1887" and is said to have been designed by Walter Lenox when he was working at Ott & Brewer. However, the jug was never copyrighted and must have been the property of several New Jersey potters. In comparison with the prices of other blanks for decorating, which ranged from a few cents to several dollars, twelve dollars was expensive. Probably few of these jugs were decorated by amateurs and those which were decorated must have been highly prized.

Although the majority of the pieces of hand-painted china available to the collector are poor in both design and painting, there was a great deal of excellent amateur china painting and good pieces must eventually come on the market. The collector should first of all look for good design and good painting. Any designs which can be traced to a known designer are interesting for a collection. Also, signed pieces even if they are not by any of the well-known painters add interest to a collection. Pieces by such men as Lycett are especially valuable as are articles marked with the name of an American manufacturer of blanks such as Ott & Brewer or Willets. Many factors enter into collecting. A piece of pottery or china may possess a shape, color, or quality of glaze which will make it attractive regardless of any attribution to a particular decorator or potter and thus, aside from its esthetic or ceramic value, some collector will be attracted to it. On the other hand many ugly pieces are collected because they are marked and thus valuable.

Although the bulk of undecorated china for amateur decorators came from abroad there were many companies in America which provided china in the plain biscuit state. Among the first was A. H. Hews and Company of Cambridge, Massachusetts. In addition to machine-made flower pots this company made a specialty of art pottery reproductions of antique Grecian, Roman, Etruscan, Phoenician and Cypriote models. They also furnished ware in the plain biscuit for decorators which was known as Albert and Albertine Ware. One of the first books published in America which included a reference to amateur pottery decoration was *Art Recreations: A Guide to Decorative Art* published by S. W. Tilton, Boston, 1877. This book includes designs and instructions for decorating Albert Ware using Flaxman's designs and Tilton's colors. This, however, was pottery, not porcelain, and never gained the popularity of china painting on porcelain. Another type of china painting which was popular with the unskilled amateur was the tinting of plaques. In 1880 Juliano Ware by Gyula de Festetics was manufactured for this purpose. It consisted of modelled plaques of lightly baked or unbaked biscuit clay which could be tinted with watercolor. The designs illustrated in the *Art Amateur*, May 1880, included Daisies, Water Lily, and Birds and Fruit Blossoms. This was not real china painting but an art recreation.

Many American pottery manufacturers furnished blanks for the serious china painter. Between 1884 and 1892 the Jersey City Pottery furnished glazed ivory white ware for decorators, including the "Worcester" vase which was a reproduction of an old pattern produced at the Worcester Works in England. Another style was called the "King" vase. These forms decorated by Edward Lycett and his son William Lycett are illustrated by Edwin Atlee Barber in *Pottery and Porcelain of the United States*. In 1887 Bawo and Dotter, dealers in chinaware in New York City, offered a price list and illustrations of over 200 items of chinaware decorated and undecorated. They sold Haviland Limoges, "Worcester and Royal Vienna for copying." Blanks included cups and saucers of various shapes, vases, creams, sugar baskets, plates, leaf and cake plates, also bone dishes, cheese dishes, and rose jars. Willets "Art Ware" for decorating included a bowl with rustic stand, wicker and shell designs. Also "Ott and Brewer Belleek to decorate beautifully." Another pottery which sold white china for decorating was the American Art China Works of Trenton, New Jersey, established in 1891. Their ware was thin, translucent and strong and resembled Belleek. Also in 1891 The Ceramic Art Company (Coxon and Lenox) advertised: "Fine Porcelains for high class decoration. Original and exclusive designs and shapes. Belleek. Pretty conceits in tableware, trays, after dinner coffees all in egg-shell china. White ware for amateur decoration." On a back page of the 1893 edition of Barber's *Pottery and Porcelain of the United States* the Knowles, Taylor & Knowles Co., East Liverpool, Ohio, advertised Lotus Ware and added this paragraph. "This ware is adapted to the requirements of amateur or professional decorators, and may be obtained usually through first-class crockery dealers. It is of a variety peculiar to itself; very pure and translucent in character, having a beautiful, soft, transparent glaze. It is made in artistic shapes designed for practical utility." Lotus Ware decorated at the pottery was marked "K.T.K. Co., Lotus Ware" with the date and initial of the decorator. The Kezonta ware of the Cincinnati Art pottery was a deep blue and white pottery made for decorators. The forms are modifications of Greek and Roman shapes and many ladies painted these for the market. The mark was "KEZ-ONTA" impressed.

Punch bowl and cups, Limoges china. Painted by George Leykauf, Detroit, Michigan. Awarded bronze medal at Columbian Exposition, 1893. (*The Henry Ford Museum*)

BOOKS FOR FURTHER READING

FURNITURE IN GENERAL

ANDREWS, EDWARD DEEMING AND FAITH, *Shaker Furniture.* Dover Publications, New York, 1937.
BAIRD, HENRY CAREY, *Cabinet Maker's Album of Furniture.* Philadelphia, 1868.
COMSTOCK, HELEN, *American Furniture.* (Studio) Viking. New York, 1962.
CONNER, ROBERT, *Cabinet Maker's Assistant.* New York, 1842.
DOWNING, ANDREW J. *Architecture of Country Houses.* New York, 1850.
EASTWOOD, CHARLES LOCKE, *Hints on Household Taste.* New York, 1872.
HALL, JOHN, *The Cabinet Maker's Assistant.* Baltimore, 1840.
KOVEL, RALPH AND TERRY, *American Country Furniture.* Crown Publishers, New York, 1965.
LEA, ZILLA RIDER, *The Ornamental Chair.* Charles E. Tuttle Co., Rutland, Vt.
MILLER, EDGAR A., JR. *American Antique Furniture* (2 vols.). (Studio) Viking. M. Barrows & Co.,
    New York, 1937.
OTTO, CELIA JACKSON, *American Furniture of the Nineteenth Century.* The Viking Press, 1965.
ROBACHER, EARL F. *Touch of the Dutchland.* A. S. Barnes & Co., Inc., 1965.
SCHWARTZ, MARVIN D., *Victoriana,* Catalogue of Loan Exhibition. Brooklyn Museum, Brooklyn, N.Y. 1960.
SMITH, WALTER, *The Masterpieces of the Centennial International Exhibition,* Vol. II, Industrial Art.
    Philadelphia, 1876.

COTTAGE FURNITURE

ANDREW J. DOWNING, *Architecture of Country Houses.* New York, 1850.
ANDREW J. DOWNING, *Cottage Residences.* New York, 1844.
Godey's Lady's Magazine, 1849 pp, 60, 132, 276.

PAPIER MÂCHÉ

Antiques Magazine, August, 1960.
MCCLINTON, KATHARINE MORRISON, *Handbook of Popular Antiques.* Random House, 1945 Bonanza, 1963.

DECORATIVE ACCESSORIES

DREPPERD, CARL W., *American Clocks & Clockmakers.* Branford.
HEYDENRYK, HENRY, *Art and History of Frames.* Jas. H. Heineman, Inc., New York, 1963.
MCCLINTON, KATHARINE MORRISON, *Antique Collecting for Everyone.* McGraw Hill, New York, 1951.
Bonanza, 1964.
PALMER, BROOKS, *American Clocks.* The Macmillan Co., New York, 1950.

ROGERS GROUPS

Rogers Groups in The New-York Historical Society by Dorothy C. Barck, *Quarterly Bulletin,* October, 1932.
Rogers Letters, Notebook, and Clippings, (7 boxes) The New-York Historical Society.

CURRIER & IVES AND OTHER LITHOGRAPHERS

PETERS, HARRY T. *Currier & Ives, Print makers to the American People,* Vols. I and II. Doubleday, Doran & Co.
PRANG, LOUIS & Co. *Catalogue,* 1876.
PRANG, LOUIS & Co. *Publishers' Proofs,* Vols. 1-15.

PRIMITIVE PAINTING

Boston Museum of Fine Arts, Maxim Karlick Collection.
FORD, ALICE, *Pictorial Folk Art New England to California.*
LIPMAN, JEAN, *American Primitive Painting.* Oxford Univ. Press. 1942.
Studio Publications, 1949.

THE VICTORIAN DINING ROOM

HARRISON, CONSTANCE GARY, *Woman's Handiwork in Modern Homes*. Charles Scribner's Sons, New York, 1881.
HIBBERD, SHIRLEY, *Rustic Ornaments for Homes of Taste*. London, 1856.
SHERMAN, ELLEN EWING, *Practical Cooking and Dinner Giving*. 1876.
SHERWOOD, MRS. JOHN, *Manners and Social Uses*. Harpers, New York, 1884.
VON FALKE, JACOB, *Art in the House*. L. Prang & Co. Boston, 1879.

GLASS

BELKNAP, E. MCCAMLY, *Milk Glass*, Crown Publishers, New York.
BERGSTROM, L. R., *Old Glass Paper Weights*. Crown Publishers.
DANIEL, DOROTHY E., *Cut and Engraved Glass*. Barrows, 1950.
KOCH, ROBERT, *Louis C. Tiffany, Rebel in Glass*. Crown Publishers, New York, 1964.
LEE, RUTH WEBB. *Early American Pressed Glass*. Lee Publishers.
MCCLINTON, KATHARINE MORRISON, *American Glass*. World Publishing Co., 1950.
MCCLINTON, KATHARINE MORRISON, *Handbook of Popular Antiques*. Random House, 1945.
MCKEARIN, GEORGE S. AND HELEN, *American Glass*. Crown Publishers, 1948.
PEARSON, J. M. AND D. T., *American Cut Glass for the Discriminating Collector*. Vantage Press, 1965.
PRESZNICK, ROSE M., *Carnival Glass Books*.
REVI, A. CHRISTIAN, *Nineteenth Century Glass*. Thos. Nelson, 1959.
REVI, A. CHRISTIAN, *American Cut and Engraved Glass*. Nelson, 1965.

SILVER AND SILVER PLATE

Art Journal, 1875, 1876
Catalogues: Reed & Barton, 1885; Meriden Britannia; James W. Tufts; Gorham & Co. (All 19th Century) Whiting & Co. Catalogue, 1895.
FREEMAN, LARRY AND BEAUMONT, JANE, *Early American Plated Silver*. Century House, Watkins Glenn, 1949.
Jewelers' Circular, 1885.
KOVEL, RALPH M. AND TERRY, *A Directory of American Silver Pewter & Silver Plate*. Crown Publishers, New York, 1961.
MCCLINTON, KATHARINE MORRISON, *The Complete Book of Small Antique Collecting*. Coward-McCann, 1965.

POTTERY AND PORCELAIN

BARBER, EDWIN ATLEE, *The Pottery and Porcelain of the United States*. G. P. Putnam, New York (1893, 1902, 1909.)
BARRET, RICHARD CARTER, *Bennington Pottery and Porcelain*. Crown Publishers, New York, 1958.
KOCH, ROBERT, *Rockwood Pottery*. Antiques Magazine, March, 1960. Rockwood Catalogue, 1904.

LADIES' HANDIWORK

CARLISLE, LILLIAN BAKER, *Pieced and Appliqué Quilts at Shelburne Museum*. Shelburne Museum.
FINLEY, RUTH, *Old Patchwork Quilts*. Lippincott, Philadelphia, 1929.
HARTLEY, FLORENCE, *Ladies' Handbook of Fancy and Ornamental Work*.
LELAND, CHARLES G., *A Manual of Wood Carving*. Art Amateur. New York, 1879–1891.
MRS. PULLAN, *Ladies' Manual of Fancy Work*. New York, 1859.
PETO, FLORENCE, *American Quilts and Coverlets*. Chanticleer Press, New York, 1949.
ROBERTSON, ELIZABETH WELLS, *American Quilts*. Studio Publications, New York, 1948.
URBINO, LEVINA, *Art Recreations*. J. F. Tilton, Boston, 1859.

CHINA PAINTING

LITTLE, RUTH, *Painting China for Pleasure and Profit*. Little, Lubbock, Texas.
MCLAUGHLIN, LOUISE, *China Painting, A Practical Manual*. New York, 1878.
PHILLIPS, L. VANCE, *Book of the China Painter*. 1896.
PITON, C., *Practical Treatise on China Painting in America*. J. Wiley & Sons, 1878.
The China Painter. New York, 1887–1900.

INDEX